Hexes and Curses Be Gone

A Witch's Guide to Destroy Witchcraft with Protection and Reversal Magick: Banishing, Eradication, and Protection Spells for Beginners

Glinda Porter

MAGICKAL
WITCHES

CONTENTS

Putting Your Magickal Wards in Place

Creating an Effective Spell

Potential Hazards When Magick Is Misused

Banishing and Eradication Spells

Spells to Destroy the Power of Negative/Harmful
Witchcraft

Spells to Break, Destroy, and Rid Negative Hexes,
Curses, and Spells

Spells to Break, Destroy, and Rid Unholy Agreements

Spells to Reverse Hexes and Curses Back to Sender

Spells for Jinx Removal

Spells to Destroy and Rid Negative/Evil Energy

Spells to Destroy and Rid Negative Entities and
Demons

Spells to Destroy and Rid Psychic Attacks

Cleansing and Manifesting Rituals

Deliverance Spells

Manifesting Fruits

Protection Spells

INTRODUCTION

The world we are living in today is all upside-down. It's hard to find peace in a world with a pandemic going on. In fact, it's downright scary. It seems people have been put under some sort of spell, adopting extreme ways of thinking and reacting from a place of fear. It is tough enough to steer clear of all the frenzied behavior. It's even tougher to feel safe in a world full of deception, greed, envy, and negativity.

Finding a way to deal with all the madness is something many people strive to achieve. People desperately want to feel safe and protected. Uncertainty makes you feel alone and finding somewhere to belong becomes crucial. Life is hard enough, and it gets worse if you're trying to take it on all by yourself.

If you try to find a place to belong and learn about how to protect yourself, you might be attracted to the notions of witchcraft. However, the topic of witchcraft has been painted with a brush of theatrics relating to witches, warlocks, spells, and more. We can thank Hollywood for that one!

(Interestingly enough, Hollywood is a conjoined word of "Holy" and "Wood," which is a direct reference to a wand!)

Back to witchcraft!

Does it work? Is it really as magical as they say? Can it help me obtain my heart's desires? There are so many questions that may be plaguing your mind. It is difficult to know what is real or what is make-believe.

Thankfully, today's youth are much more informed and curious. Young witches have opened up a huge online door to the world of magick and witchcraft. The idea of burning witches at the stake has been losing ground to the idea of acceptance. More importantly, the old-timey religious views of witchcraft are quickly fading into the pages of history.

While people are more interested in practicing the occult—which includes witchcraft, sorcery, astral projection, energy work, and much more—there is just so much to discover. What does it take to be a witch? What do they do? Do I need to be born a witch?

In essence, witchcraft is nothing more than the belief and practice of magick. While magick can be defined in many ways, for the sake of this book, we will simply define it as "exerting one's will onto the universe." Certain aspects like making potions, practicing divination, or spell works all form part of being a witch.

If you decide to walk this path, it's important to get to know the craft. Read up as much as you can about all the aspects of witchcraft. One of the first valuable differentiations you need to know is that magick and magic are not the same. Magic is stage-oriented, used for card tricks and illusions. As mentioned, magick is a spiritual practice where we direct our intent and energy, and engage with the very nature of reality!

Interesting side note: "Magic" was created by mages to disguise real witches and sorcerers, as anyone who practiced real magick was persecuted during the Crusades. Real witches of the time created things like Tarot cards, which encapsulate many esoteric truths, to convince their oppressors they were merely performing "parlor tricks" when in reality, they were engaging in sorcery and witchcraft.

In the beginning, it is hard to know which path to follow. That is why it is a good idea to research many of the different paths available. It helps to identify your "why" behind pursuing this path. Are you seeking to protect yourself? Do you want to ward off negativity? Are spells the way you want to go, and if so, which ones work?

Maybe you're interested in the power of crystals or how the phases of the moon influence everything. As you dive into this rabbit hole, jot down the particular practices you align with most. In other words, find out what resonates with you personally. Ultimately, witchcraft is a personal journey of engaging with the world!

In these uneasy times, many people are seeking to find themselves and belong somewhere. It's a time when many people are reinventing themselves. During this process of self-reinvention, it's important to approach concepts with an open mind—to permit yourself to be surprised! We are definitely at a turning point on earth.

The old rigid ways and dualistic traditions are falling from public favor. We are beginning to see the erosion of institutions that stood as "pillars of society" for thousands of years.

We are seeing that which was thought to be "unbreakable, unshakeable, and permanent" begin to crumble. There has emerged a deeper need for spiritual independence in a world where corporations and governments can spy on you and sell your data to the highest bidder.

The norms of morality are waning and people are beginning to construct their own belief systems. This is especially true when it comes to practicing magick. It's also the reason why following the path of practicing magick is so alluring.

If you have made the decision to become a "practicing witch" and decided to deepen your knowledge on the subject matter, then the first recommendation is to start a Book of Shadows. This book will become your closest friend. The Book of Shadows is your journal where you keep track of everything you learn. You keep track of spells and your magickal workings. You will note everything that forms part of your path in this book.

This is something most experienced witches recommend to people who choose the path of witchcraft—no matter the current you follow. There are no specific rules. You create it your way. You decide what works for you and what does not. Once you have created your Book of Shadows, the next obvious step is learning spell work.

However, is it possible to just jump in and learn spells to protect yourself? Are there any inherent dangers of practicing magick? These are just some of the topics we'll explore in more detail in this book. There are some dangers, but for the most part, practicing witchcraft is simply about exerting will onto the universe. Just remember, mastering something takes time and dedication, and over time, your magick becomes more consistent.

Other than what is presented in the media and movies, a witch is just someone who understands the innate power she or he has and how to effectively use it for their benefit. Practicing magick is also simply knowing how to direct energy to complete your intention. Most people cast spells all the time without knowing it.

This is because we all ultimately possess the power to direct energy, whether physically utilizing our bodies or directing our emotions and thoughts. There are no inherent dangers to this practice, yet when you begin to venture into the world of hexes and curses, there are things to consider.

Keep in mind that as with anything we do, casting spells and practicing magick comes with a price. One could even say "more so" when dealing with hexing someone. As you continue reading, you'll quickly realize that the focus of this book is all about learning how to protect yourself against negative witchcraft and spells, like how to identify a curse or a hex and how to deal with it adequately.

We are powerful beings with more punch in our words and thoughts than we know. It's possible to unintentionally put a curse on someone else or even yourself by simply uttering a word or a sentence. Negative thoughts—and more so, dwelling on them—can lead to even cursing yourself. As a witch, you understand these principles, and begin to modify your words and deeds accordingly.

I believe every one of us has, at one time or another, felt we were under a curse. What we don't know is that sometimes this curse was due to our own dark thoughts. However, a negative attitude from someone else towards you could also be the cause. By practicing witchcraft, you will begin to understand the origins of these phenomena, and in turn, can learn to deal with it effectively. Knowledge is powerful. Learning how to use it even better. Believing in your own ability will be the first step in our process. This is what this book hopes to achieve.

I believe we all are born with the ability to practice witchcraft.

Since I was a child, I have had the ability to perceive entities in dreams. Coming from a more traditional family, it was never picked up on or developed. Rather, it was seen as a threat, and for years, I was very closed off to understanding the spiritual world and energies around me.

But "somehow," I also "knew" stuff. I now know this is called Divination.

I would know where I would end up living as a grown-up. It was to be on a completely different continent. I knew how many children I would have, and in what sequence.

Only later, I discovered the connection I have to crystals and the energy that resonates from them. How I was drawn to them has sparked my interest even more. I studied up on them, beginning to understand how their frequencies resonate with our energy and how they can be used for healing and protection.

Over the years, I began deepening my understanding of these elements and putting my magick into practice. I realized I could divine and cast spells—that is, use stones and herbs to cast protection spells and much more. This lifestyle has led me down many different paths, learning many different occult secrets.

Now that I look back on the mistakes and false beliefs I harbored for so long—and the general lack of good information on the subject—I decided to write this book to help young witches along their path.

Finding your path and learning how to use magick to protect yourself and cast off negative energy is all inside you. As I said above, there are no specific paradigms under which you must operate. Most practitioners use various elements of different witchcraft currents within their own practices. The most important is to find what corresponds to your own liking, and how to practice and strengthen it.

An uncertain road only becomes clear when you enlighten yourself! Throughout this book, you'll uncover many different elements to help you define your practice and keep you safe!

Quick Recommendation from the Magickal Witches team:

We would like to make the magickal journey you are about to embark on as smooth as possible. As with any journey, preparations need to be made, and there are tools fit for each witch, new or experienced.

In our case, we'd like to recommend the "Survival and Wellness Kit for Magickal Witches", which is completely free. Not using these tools is like making a trip to a rainforest and not taking any sort of tool to protect yourself from mosquitoes. You can do it, but the experience won't be quite as seamless as it could have been. It's discomfort that's not necessary and can be prevented. This analogy fits perfectly; if you don't have the right tools to go through with this process, it can be uncomfortable, and there is even a risk of not having a practice full of magick.

Besides, it's just an awesome free gift! Please, see for yourself. You won't regret it!

Scan the QR code to get inside the Magickal Witches toolkit for:

- 10 Elixirs For Detoxification and Aura Cleansing

- 12 Spell Jar Recipes For Protection

- Guide For Talisman Preparation For Use Outside Home

- 20 Daily Detox Tips To Keep Your Vessel Clear

- Master Ingredient Shopping List

It may not be completely clear why these components are essential quite yet, but in further chapters, you will notice that this information will be very helpful. When you actually begin the practical side of the magickal work, you will come to understand. These tools are meant to alleviate some stress and obstacles that may show up along the way. For the time being, let's dive into understanding some theories that are meant to enhance the magickal journey you're here for.

1

— . —

Part i – Understanding, Knowing, and Signs

What Is a Spell?

In the simplest form, a spell is an "intention" made manifest.

Ultimately, if you are casting a spell, you are simply exerting a desired "outcome" onto the universe. It's a projection of sorts that is reinforced by a deep-rooted "belief" that it is working. The universe then accommodates itself to sustain this belief. If you are under a spell, then you believe the conditions of the intention and subscribe to the paradigm—that is, your thoughts and actions are dictated by the spell.

Spells can be simple, and they can be complex. Some of them can be casted by simply uttering words whereas others require rituals to conjure.

However, experienced witches know that casting a spell might not always be the best course of action. Often, ordinary solutions deal with a problem just as fast and require less energy. For example, you could try to summon a spirit guide to fix the leaky faucet or call a plumber.

Sure, a spirit guide and a plumber might share many similar qualities—it simply requires less focused energy to conjure a plumber!

Spells can be traced back to ancient times. There are many different grimoires out there that whisper the roots of magick. There are many different methods of casting: it could be spoken, be a gesture, or something else, like sigils or a wand.

Spells can be just a sentence, or they can consist of a very complicated ritual. Spells can be done by using crystals, candles, or plants. However, the main intention stays the same: we want to bring something that doesn't exist into existence through will, belief, and energy.

So, in plain words: a spell is desire, intent, faith, and energy focused on a particular outcome!

Energy plays a vital role in a spell. The more focused the energy, the better the outcome. We typically try to utilize high-frequency emotions like joy, love, pleasure, happiness, anger, hate, etc. However, things can get a bit unpredictable when casting from a place of anger or hate. Therefore, most witches prefer to utilize lighter emotions as fuel for their spells.

While I'm providing you with these definitions, the truth is that spell work grows with you over time. Right now, you're learning the theory of magick, but once you have had a few successes, your mind will understand that "non-linear engagement" is very possible. You'll begin to "see" how your energy impacts the universe!

Everything is energy.

Science has proven this fact over and over again. This is why spell work can be seen as a form of energy based in science. Energy cannot be destroyed or created, but it can be captured and redirected.

With the correct intention, energy is harnessed and redirected to create a new reality. The energy we use comes from the natural world around us. It's advisable to use these external sources for energy while it's possible to draw energy from yourself—it can take a toll on your body.

The elements of nature, crystals, colors, herbs, etc., are all filled with energy we can use. If we can learn to vibrate at the energy levels we desire, we can bring it to us.

How Do You Do That?

Let's talk about the mechanisms of magick. First, you need to find the corresponding link between you and the desired energy. A simple example is lighting a candle to manifest something like love in your life. The candle by itself doesn't do anything; it is merely a conduit. However, if you choose a pink candle and you think of pink resembling love and everything related to it, this object now helps raise your energy levels. This result is because our unconscious mind creates a psychic link to the candle, instructing our higher self to make it so.

The unconscious mind works in symbols and not words—this is why these objects become "magickal." These are symbols and metaphors our deep minds use to move energy accordingly.

Over time and with practice, your energy levels will get higher. Learning what object resonates on what level also helps in the process. Every object or color emits a frequency. Finding the right object or color to resonate with what you desire makes it easier for the higher self to connect to the desire.

There is more than enough collective information on stones, colors, herbs, elements, and more to help you find objects to work with. Studying up on these properties will also help you connect with your deep desires, facilitating the process of casting a spell and exerting your will onto the universe.

However, spells come in many shapes and sizes. Just as spells can be positive, they can also be baneful. In the instance of baneful magick, spells are cast to counter the effect, or bind it. Spells can also alter the negative desired effect directed at you or someone else. That is why intention and focus are so important in spell-casting, and being clear about the outcome even more so.

What Is a Hex and a Curse?

Whenever we hear about a curse or a hex, it refers to negative magick. It is also named "dark" or "black" magick. In simple terms, curses can be performed by anyone knowingly or unknowingly. Hexes are performed by someone practicing witchcraft.

A curse can be very harmful and can even last for generations. In certain cases, it can also be inherited by offspring. It has been with humankind since the beginning. Some practitioners believe it is possible to not include curses as part of your path. But the existence of curses cannot be denied.

The terms hex and curse are mostly seen as the same kind of thing, as they come from the same type of magick. But there are slight differences between them. The focus is the same in that both intend a negative outcome towards either a person or a specific situation.

Often, curses are more purposefully cast whereas hexes sometimes happen because of strong emotional energy channeled toward a person. It doesn't imply that hexes can't be purposefully cast, but they are generally more temporary.

Specifically, What Is a Hex?

The word "hex" can be used as a verb or a noun, which means it can be transitive or intransitive. A hex is considered evil because it intends for a bad thing to happen. It normally has a temporary effect.

It comes from the German word "hexen" that means witchcraft. Because it is less harmful, it never is fatal. However, hexes can be harsh as they hit hard and fast, but they generally disappear after a time. In contrast, curses can endure for generations.

Common types of hexes are:

- Creating distance between people with the intention to hurt them or make them feel solitude.

- Let someone feel regret for a particular action they incurred against you.

- Preventing someone from finding love.

- Destroying hope or faith in something.

A hex usually influences only one aspect of your life, like your health or relationship. Therefore, if you have a sudden spell of bad luck in one aspect of your life, you most likely have had a hex cast on you. If you do nothing, you may experience hardship for a time, but just as suddenly, the hardship will disappear.

Specifically, What Is a Curse?

Perhaps at one time you became so angry at someone, you lashed out at them in a heightened state of emotion. In your anger, you may have blurted out that the person goes to hell or that their physical health is compromised in one way or another.

Afterwards, you may feel better, but the reality is, you actually cursed the person. Often, a curse is said in anger. But the deeper the resentment or hatred for a person or thing, the stronger the intention.

Curses can come from anywhere. Intentional curses are more likely to be linked to dark magick, but it is just as common in religious practices. A curse is super-intense and can cross over many aspects of your life. You might suffer misfortune in many areas, as though a blanket of misery has covered your life.

It can also focus on one specific aspect of your life. The difference between curses and hexes is that curses will linger for a very long time. If a person can't remove the curse by themselves, it has to be removed by someone experienced.

What If You Curse Someone?

Practitioners are often concerned that a curse can come back to you. This is because in order to cast on someone else, you have to envision the curse happening. This dark visualization is an internal process, and so the "target" you are visualizing in the moment is actually you. After all, the "other" person doesn't exist in your mind—that is a part of you masquerading as "them."

Thus, when cursing or hexing someone, you are firstly cursing and hexing yourself—or the "image of another within yourself"—and then releasing that energy into the universe. If done improperly, the curse can linger in your own psyche, and you can begin to experience some of the curse's qualities in your own life.

Reciprocity within magick is a real thing, and wherever you focus your attention, energy flows! If you aren't able to successfully banish the curse from your own mind, you'll begin to focus on its effects—and as mentioned, the "image in your mind" is you! Then, the law of attraction kicks in. What you sow, you will reap.

Experienced practitioners will tell you to practice the rule of three. Whatever energy a person puts out into the world will come back three times; it doesn't matter if it is positive or negative energy. But this rule is never as clear-cut as that.

Common Types of Curses

There are so many types of curses, it would be impossible to name them all. It depends on the intention, motive, and condition.

Direct curses can be distinguished by:

- Feelings of hatred and anger

- Envy and jealousy

- Competition—against the competitor

- To influence welfare

- To protect objects

This list is just scraping the surface. Curses is such a vast topic to cover, it would need a book by itself. We will be diving deeper into types of curses and how to counter them later in this book.

Understanding Generational Hexes and Curses

Generational curses are passed from one generation to another. A generational curse is often casted generations ago (hence the name), so it is not easy to pinpoint the exact time of origin. It can be carried over from either side of the family.

It can also skip a generation. To make it even more complicated, it can skip specific people in the generation; meaning, not everyone experiences the curse. It's most often noticed when one person has the same physical illness as another from one generation to the next or experiences similar "luck" as someone from the past.

A generational curse can manifest itself in the spiritual, physical, or mental realm of the person's existence. It always relates to negative behavioral patterns from one generation to the next. For example, if a family struggles with alcoholism for generations, that could very well be a generational curse!

Physical manifestation – these are curses on a genetic level where certain medical conditions like heart problems, diabetes, and cancers continue to manifest from one generation to the next.

Environmental manifestation – behavioral issues, like self-destructive behavior, are learned behavioral patterns. We learn a lot from our family, and such patterns are also carried over. Such generational curses could be divorce, poverty, and broken relationships.

Mental manifestation – mental illnesses and addictions can also be due to generational curses.

Curses can originate from different places. Sometimes, it can be as simple as someone saying, "You'll always be poor and so will your family!" When the receiver of the curse integrates the instruction into their psyche, it is a curse that can last a very long time. This curse is regarded as negative witchcraft, even when done unintentionally.

If you notice all the men in your family over generations never get to be successful, or end up in jail because of bad behavior, it could be a sign of a generational curse. Or, most of the women in your family might be prone to abortion or still births. That, too, could be a generational curse.

Understanding Negative Soul Ties, Covenants, and Agreements

Negative Soul Ties

Soul ties refer to a link between two people's souls. A soul tie can be good or bad, but for the purpose of this book, we will focus on negative soul ties.

When a soul tie is negative, it bonds one person to another, whether they like it or not. An example of an unhealthy soul tie would be when an abused woman is drawn to a man she would normally avoid. No matter how badly he treats her, she simply can't "escape" his allure.

Most soul ties are formed due to physical relationships. But emotional, spiritual, and social relationships can also lead to soul ties. When we speak about sexual relationships forming negative soul ties, it refers to the other person's bad energies and traumas mixing with your energy, too. This soul tie can manifest in many different ways in your life.

How Do You Know You Have a Negative Soul Tie?

The first sign of a negative soul tie is when you are just not able to break a relationship. Every time you decide to break up and pack your bags, you change your mind. It's not a normal decision; it's as if something keeps you trapped. As hard as you try to leave, it's just impossible!

The second sign is when the person with whom you are having a relationship is constantly on your mind. Even though you know the relationship is bad for you, the moment you decide to break away and do something good for yourself, the person still comes into your mind. You stop what you were going to do and think instead of how you can do something for that person. You simply can't break away because something will be missing if you do. Your souls are tied together.

The third sign is when you can't do anything without the approval of the other person. It's as if you are under the control of that person. You are afraid to think for yourself because the other person might not like what you want to do. The knot is so tight, you can't function by yourself.

The fourth sign is when whatever happens to the other person happens to you. When the person feels sick, you feel sick. You two are so aligned, you are almost the same person. You don't even have to be in the same room with the other person.

The fifth sign is when you get so dependent on the other person, you don't think of yourself as an individual anymore. You can't do anything alone anymore. You always think of what to do with the other person.

These are just rudimentary examples to give you an idea how soul ties work.

Covenants

A covenant is something that comes from the beginning of recorded history, and probably even before then. It is an oath-bound agreement between two or more parties. On a human level, something like marriage could be seen as a covenant. On the divine level, a covenant is formed between deities and their followers.

There are always conditions to a covenant. When the covenant is broken, there are consequences. These consequences can be quite severe and even lead to death.

Negative covenants often have ingredients of manipulation, intimidation, and dominance without any real benefits for the other party.

Be careful not to form part of a covenant that would ultimately feel like total control. When free will is taken out of the equation, it spells danger.

Agreements

Commonly speaking, witches are known to make pacts, contracts, or agreements with spiritual entities to obtain power and magickal knowledge. Like this, it was told for hundreds of years. It is still practiced in modern-day witchcraft where relationships are established for self-enlightenment. In a more "formal tone," agreements are referred to as "pacts" where an agreement between two different beings from two different worlds is established. The respect between the two beings should be equal and mutual, otherwise you enter into a "dark pact."

There can be many agreements, and some could be unspoken. Just as in a society where there is an unspoken agreement on how to react, contribute, and participate effectively, in witches' covens and circles, there are also more established agreements and unspoken forms of engagement.

With a conscious mind, a magickal practitioner should look at the agreements he or she is entering. In agreements with entities, it is easy to become a servant to the greater power of the entity. What you are offering must be clear, and just as clear must be the role of the entity. In any case, the end goal of the agreement should be working together. There should also be a definite end to the agreement, something that says, "We are done when X, Y or Z happens."

Ideally, you should never function as a servant in an agreement, but rather, provide a service.

Understanding Psychic Attacks

Psychic attacks are more common than we want to believe. The general public might not be aware of the negative energies around them and how these energies can influence them. But those operating in the occult definitely know about the powers out there and the effect they can have.

The Witch's Shield by Christopher Penczak says: "Psychic attack is much like a curse, but it is done by one who is not necessarily using the tools of ritual magick."

Those sensitive to energy are more likely to experience psychic attacks, but they can happen to anyone. Just like when our immune systems are low and we are vulnerable to physical illness, our mental energy can also be vulnerable.

Knowingly or unknowingly, we can open ourselves to such attacks. When our energy levels are high, we aren't easy targets. But if someone has an unhealthy admiration for your abilities, or explicitly wants to do you harm, he or she can send low vibrational energy (baneful intentions) to fulfill the lack they feel in themselves.

A psychic attack can affect a person on every plane—physical, emotional, or spiritual.

Signs you might be under a psychic attack:

- Feeling tired and physically drained all the time, almost lethargic.

- You feel nauseous all the time and experience severe headaches for no reason at all.

- Mentally, you feel foggy and keep forgetting stuff.

- You lack joy.

- You feel spiritually "off."

- You feel as if you are being watched by something creepy and evil.

- You hear voices or have fearful dreams.

- You have constant thoughts of a specific person in your mind.

- You are suddenly accident-prone.

- You start losing stuff you normally don't.

If you experience any of the above, or any other weird and sudden change, you can very well be under a psychic attack. Sometimes, psychic attacks can even come from people you consider friends. For example, if someone is jealous of a new job you obtained, they could be envisioning how you fail miserably at your new venture. This envious energetic signature directed at you is a psychic attack!

Dangers of Witchcraft

While we said earlier that witchcraft in essence isn't a "dangerous activity," it does have some inherent dangers. Witchcraft has been widely practiced over all cultures for many years. As humankind began, so did witchcraft. It is believed that witchcraft involves the supernatural and focuses on crafting spells and practicing rituals.

Different cultures have different viewpoints on witchcraft. In some cultures, witchcraft is seen as evil and malignant. In other cultures, it is embraced and seen as acceptable for healing and protecting people.

Today, modern witchcraft is often viewed as practicing magick on a neutral metaphysical level by using meditation, self-help techniques, and divination.

Witchcraft is a massive topic with many different paths. One of these paths also includes dark magick. When magick becomes malicious and harmful, it can spell out danger in your life or those of intended targets.

When the aim of your witchcraft is controlling and manipulating others, we consider this to be baneful magick. Curses, dark or black magic, and dark occult intent to harm are still very much part of society. You'd be surprised by how many billionaires consult witches for protection and prosperity.

However, apart from using witchcraft to harm someone, when it is used for selfish reasons and personal gain, it can also be seen as baneful. For example, there are many witches who prey on the vulnerable by pretending to break curses or spells when in reality they are simply "milking their customers." If there is a lack of sincerity, then there can be negative consequences in your life and those of your "customers."

Practices like tarot reading, spiritual healing, deliverance, and clairvoyance are all great tools for the practicing witch. But there are also many scammers out there who take advantage of the gullible. Scammers are part of the reason why you should study these things yourself—to master these crafts.

If you start practicing witchcraft, and you feel uneasy or fearful when you are with other practitioners, the best thing to do is step away. Not all witches have good intentions. More importantly, not all those who practice magick are indeed "practicing witches."

Types of Witchcraft and Curses

For many ignorant people, witchcraft relates to dark magick. It generally is referred to as the occult. However, the word "occult" literally means "hidden." Yes, curses are real and fall under witchcraft, but not all forms of witchcraft use curses as their main focus. There are too many different types of witchcraft or curses to address all of them here. As previously mentioned, diving into the deep pool of witchcraft is intense and eye-opening. Arming yourself with information and finding the path corresponding to your interest will ultimately guide you on your way.

Different Types of Witchcraft

We will look at some paths that might be more known. But again, there are many paths.

1. Traditional Witchcraft

Even starting with traditional witchcraft makes it difficult to define it. Those calling themselves "traditional" are limited to their ideas of what it means to be "traditional." Depending on the culture, traditional witchcraft can take many different forms.

The main aspect of this type of witchcraft is that it is based on tradition of a particular culture or sect. The spells, rituals, and belief systems are passed on from generation to generation. Some witches will also take on an acolyte to train; this way, the "current" is passed down, even if it isn't their own kin.

These witches typically tend to have deep knowledge of herbs and stones. Also, they likely have a few grimoires in their magickal library.

2. Wiccan Witchcraft

Some refer to Wiccan witchcraft as a religion. Wiccans have a well-established belief system that includes the practice of witchcraft. However, Wiccans can choose not to practice witchcraft but still be considered Wiccan by following the spiritual path and the Wiccan Rede.

Wicca is strongly connected to the seasons and their cycles. It is also different from other belief systems in that Wiccans have a female deity. This religion considers equal status to males and females, making it one of their most important principles. The Rede is also an essential part of Wiccan spell-crafting in that it is used to limit spells. The Rede promotes positive morality and a strong philosophy for many practicing witches.

You don't necessarily need to be part of a coven to be considered Wicca; you must simply follow the philosophy and principles of the practice.

3. Green Witchcraft

Green witchcraft is rooting witchcraft in nature and the elements thereof. It springs from ancestral healing with herbs handed down for generations. Green witches use energy from plants, herbs, and crystals for therapeutic and magickal purposes.

Because a green witch's path is connected to nature, she or he fully understands the natural energy of earth.

For a green witch, taking care of plants is part of their practice, which plays an important role relating to the ingredients needed for this particular spell-crafting. Also, maintaining balanced energy with the earth is also very important. Herbs, spices, flowers, and trees are all critical components in these witches' practice. Their energy and properties together with herbs and plants are valuable to these witches' work.

The cycles of the seasons and the phases of the moon also form a part of this current. These patterns are essential in gaining knowledge of the earth's movement.

4. Kitchen Witchcraft

This type of witchcraft literally takes place right at home. It's surrounded by homely aspects in the kitchen and involves a lot of cooking. However, it's more than just cooking, as while cooking, magick can be infused for healing or whatever spell is involved. An ordinary cup of tea can be infused with magick, for example.

What makes a kitchen witch different from an ordinary cook is the intention behind the cooking. There is a deep connection to each ingredient; it doesn't matter if it is plant or animal-based.

A kitchen witch normally sets up their workplace to avoid clutter. Unnecessary items and energies are removed. The kitchen becomes their place of spell-crafting, with each meal imbued with intention.

5. Hearth Witchcraft

Hearth witchcraft intersects with green witchcraft and kitchen witchcraft. All the energies are connected with the magic of home. Hearth witchcraft dates back to when every village had a healer and counselor. The magick gets woven into household items such as candles, knitted products, sewing, and everything the practitioner finds grounding.

Hearth witches like to explore their creativity and can use literally anything to form part of their practice.

6. Hedge Witchcraft

A hedge witchcraft practitioner also has a strong relationship with earth and nature as he or she works with herbal magick. Hedge witches also frequently work with different deities.

Hedge witchcraft is usually a solitary path, and hedge witches see themselves as a link between the present and the past. They are deeply connected to otherworldly deities and entities. Home is normally seen as sacred, and a lot of focus is on herbal conjuring and aromatherapy. Most plants would be harvested by themselves in order to maintain the purity of the energy surrounding each element. They are considered deeply spiritual.

In the olden days, these witches would normally be found on the outskirts of the village or town.

7. Water Witchcraft

Sea witches are something many people know about. But you don't necessarily have to live close to the sea to be a water witch. Any person who feels drawn to water can practice water witchcraft. Often, such people live close to a large body of water like a river, lake, or ocean. It is normal for a water witch to be very powerful and follow a solitary path.

Water is one of the elements and a very strong force. Humans are made up mostly of water, and without water, life cannot exist. Scientifically, it is proven that energy can alter a water molecule. A water witch utilizes this principle to enact change in consensus reality.

As with traditional witchcraft, no practitioner of water witchcraft practices equally. Water is filled with all sorts of creatures and organisms that, combined with magick, create powerful spells, potions, and curses.

Any form of water can be used as a conduit for magickal intention. Water is part of many fundamental spiritual practices. Water witches can use any object related to water—seashells, beach sand, elements from swamps, rivers—to connect to water to carry their magick.

8. Cultural Witchcraft

Cultural witchcraft traditions are something many witches link and incorporate into their practice. Each culture has its own mythology, myths, deities of the pantheon, and folklore that can be drawn upon.

As cultural traditions are so broad, there will also be many differences when it comes to witchcraft. Most witches draw on what feels closest spiritually from their culture of origin. For this reason, African witches will greatly differ from European-based witches or Asian witches.

9. Eclectic Witchcraft

Eclectic witchcraft has no specific path to follow. These witches follow whatever corresponds to them. They draw from different elements, beliefs, and magickal systems. Their main focus is tailoring their practices to their specific preferences and needs.

They tend to follow their intuition to find their spiritual path. They don't use labels too often. They can be part of one belief system, but follow another deity from other belief systems. Almost every witch starts their path as an eclectic witch until they find the specific path they correspond with.

10. Secular Witchcraft

These witches often are looked at as a form of lower witchcraft. No spirituality or religion is used in their practices.

While they do cast spells, they don't believe in the spiritual energy behind it. They will use herbs, crystals, oils, and candles, but there is no spirituality whatsoever.

These witches typically employ energy as their main mechanism for delivering magickal intent.

11. Air Witchcraft

This witchcraft is practiced by witches strongly connected to the air element. Air becomes their conduit to manifest magickal intent. These witches can use any form of air elements, like incense magick or their own breath. They can choose to work with deities connected to the air, any air element, or elemental spirit. Air witchcraft is a very specific practice, and not many practice this witchcraft.

12. Cosmic Witchcraft

The practitioners following this path work primarily with planetary or cosmic energies. They work very closely with the cycles of the moon, solar, and planetary energies. These witches are deeply connected to astrology and the placement of the planets, particularly interested in how they affect our lives.

Additionally, major cosmic events are typically used for major rituals and spell work. Things like full moons, blood moons, comets, etc., all form part of this current of witchcraft.

13. Crystal Witchcraft

Crystals can be used in other forms of witchcraft, but those specializing in this current primarily focus on crystals as conduits for magick. Almost everything these witches do in their practice involves crystals in one way or another. They can meditate with crystals, use them for healing, or use them as talismans. They also use crystals in their altars or as offerings.

Crystal witches place a heavy emphasis on any type of stones and, in a way, could be considered "earth witches," considering all crystals and stones come from the earth.

14. Draconic Witchcraft

Draconic witches work only with dragon energy. They call on dragon spirits by invoking or evoking them in performing ritual and spell work. They do draconic meditations and even astral traveling to encounter spiritual entities that embody dragon magick. Draconic witches always work closely with their own kin, with whom they connect on spiritual and magickal levels.

15. Elemental Witchcraft

These practitioners use all the elements and effectively incorporate them into their work. That is, they use any or all of the four elements in their rituals and spells. These witches tend to draw power from the air, fire, earth, or water and utilize their energies to effect change on reality.

We consider these witches more "generalists" compared to witches working with only one element, but they rarely do a spell without calling on at least one of the elements.

16. Fairy Witchcraft

This type of witchcraft specializes in the Fae. Practitioners will have fairy gardens outside their homes. In all their work, they call on the spirits of the fairies and their kin. It is common practice to leave offerings for them, and some even travel to the fairy realm to work their magick from there.

These witches can work in both realms and hardly ever do any magick without the Fae's assistance.

17. Hereditary Witchcraft

In this current of witchcraft, the witch inherits everything carried down through the generations.

They are born into witchcraft and are taught by members of their family. Because of this, hereditary witches have a great arsenal of spells, recipes, and rituals to draw from. They have a very exclusive practice.

They can also tap into the power of their ancestors to help their craft.

18. Lunar Witchcraft

In lunar witchcraft, witches have a very deep connection to lunar energy. They work with moon phases in their spells and rituals. Their crystals are charged by moonlight, and everything they do perfectly aligns with the particular lunar energy for the spell. They draw their energy solely from the moon. It's a very specific witchcraft.

19. Pop-Culture Witchcraft

This type of witchcraft draws on pop-culture references within their magickal work. They get their inspiration from things like Harry Potter or Sabrina the Teenage Witch and creatively swirl it into their work. They make fantasy part of their real-life practice.

Within this particular current of witchcraft, practitioners believe in the archetypal energies associated with the pop-culture reference. The collective belief and attention of the masses imbues these entities with actual power. A pop-culture witch then taps into that power and utilizes it to effect change.

20. Sigil Witchcraft

The practitioners of sigil witchcraft use sigils in every aspect of their magick. A sigil is a symbolic representation of one's intent. They use any form of sigils, including simply drawing them on a piece of paper and then burning them, or very complicated sigils requiring magickal tools like incense or candles. All their energy is focused on one single sigil. Sigil witchcraft can be a very powerful and quick form of witchcraft.

There are many ways to make sigils, and every practitioner will refine their technique to suit their personality. It is becoming a more popular form of witchcraft as sigils are becoming easier to find. There are even online sigil makers.

21. Spirit Witchcraft

Often, different witchcraft practices make use of spiritual energies, but some witches prefer to be called spirit workers. They use single or multiple spirits in their work. These types of witches normally have altars for either one or multiple spirits and can connect to ancestral spirits or spirits of their choice.

These witches often put out offerings like wine, water, or special food in honor of the spirit. This act is meant to gain favor in the eyes of the entity who, in turn, would be working on the behalf of the practitioner.

22. Tech or Cyber Witchcraft

As the name indicates, practitioners of tech witchcraft use technology to do their work. They practice their magick from their phones or computers. Everything from their Book of Shadows, spells, rituals, and recipes are stored on their devices. They even have digital altars. They draw everything from technology.

This is a very convenient form of witchcraft and is a newer, emerging current.

23. Urban Witchcraft

Urban witches work with traditional ideas, but use their urban environment to their best advantage. They charge sigils on very busy corners. They use water from the drain to cast curses and hexes. They use the elements around them to manipulate energy and use it in their magick.

Urban witchcraft is fairly new since more people live in city-like environments than before. These witches no longer have access to green areas or open areas, so they use what they have to their best ability.

24. Luciferian Witchcraft

In Luciferian witchcraft, the focus is mainly on enlightenment, independence, and human progress. These witches' altars are built to enhance selfhood and self-awareness. They also connect to the ancient masters who were non-theistic.

They believe that gods, demons, and spirits are all personifications of what exist within individuals as well as in nature.

These kinds of witches also believe that humans created the gods and deities in their image to bring order to the natural world. They believe their actions are guided by themselves. Whatever tool they choose to practice magick or cast spells should be utilized to cultivate the power within self—ultimately the greatest power one can obtain, according to their belief system.

They use their altars as a charging station to focus their intent. The items on the altar should truly resonate and have meaning to the person. This altar then becomes the conduit for their magick.

There are many more types of witchcraft currents out there. The above is only a small look into some of the paths. We haven't looked into dark magick or black magick at all, for instance.

Finally, as mentioned before, no single practitioner immediately knows what type of path she or he wants to follow. Many of the paths blend into one another and mix different elements of specific paths.

The more you practice, the easier it becomes to identify which specific current or elements of a current most resonate with you.

Different Types of Curses

Instead of the word curse, there are other words like malediction, execration, doom, misfortune, calamity, affliction, torment, and so forth. Each word indicates the opposite of goodness. When a person experiences any misfortune in his or her life, there might be a curse on that person. However, it's also important to note that sometimes you can just experience old-fashioned "bad luck."

So, misfortune is not always a curse! Being able to tell the difference between bad luck and a curse is of paramount importance.

There are many different manifestations of curses. Some are directed to people whereas others are directed to objects. For example, cursing an object such as "treasure" is meant to protect it from someone else. The curse is ineffective to the caster; however, if anyone else attempts to steal it, the curse would manifest itself.

Nonetheless, understanding these different manifestations will provide you with the foundation to combat them in the future.

Let's look at different types of curses.

1. Generational Curses

We have already addressed generational curses, so we won't go too deeply into this type of curse again. In short, generational curses are carried over from one generation to another. It's hard to establish when it was set in motion. It sometimes affects many family members, and sometimes, it skips a generation.

2. Verbal Curses

A person can curse someone else merely by using words. It often happens out of anger. The amount of energy behind the words is enough to have the desired effect.

Screaming "F%*k you!" to someone in anger is called "cursing" because you are utilizing mal-intent with heightened emotion. This could be a reactionary curse. It can also be intentional, where the motive is to harm the person. When a curse is laid by a person in authority, it is thought to have even more power. This is because people tend to place more importance on the words of authority figures.

Sometimes, a curse happens knowingly, but other times, an authoritative figure like a parent or a teacher can cast harmful curses. For example, if a teacher calls you "lazy" or "dumb," this, too, can be a verbal curse.

You can even curse yourself. We are taught to watch our words. It's not for no reason, because if we repetitively speak negative words to ourselves, we curse ourselves. Where your focus lies, energy will flow!

3. Earned Curses (Karmic Curses)

These types of curses are what you brought upon yourself. It reflects on something that the person did to deserve a curse. These curses may be invoked through visceral actions such as rape and murder, or breaking something that is consecrated and holy. Sometimes, it can be due to a curse intended for someone else backfiring. As mentioned earlier, casting baneful magick can be dangerous to the self.

These curses can be obtained knowingly or obliviously. In many cases, you'll need a "curandero" or some form of witch doctor to help remove these spells.

Signs to Know You Are Under Witchcraft Attack

Many people believe they are cursed. Nothing goes right for them. Bad luck sticks to them like a nasty piece of chewing gum they simply can't get rid of. It feels like good fortune is never going to befall them ever again.

As we mentioned earlier, bad luck might simply be the chaotic nature of the universe expressing itself. Oftentimes, your tribulations are meant as a springboard into new realities—this doesn't mean you are cursed. It simply means the universe is testing your resolve.

To cast a curse is no joke. It takes a very skilled practitioner to cast a curse, and it comes with a cost. Casting a curse requires a lot of energy and a great deal of anger, resentment, and other negative emotions. The problem is that the energy being released comes back, which means that negative energy from the one being cursed affects the one casting the curse.

That's why deliberate curses are not such a common thing whereas undeliberate curses are everywhere!

Therefore, it's always best to first look at all the mundane reasons why something isn't working as opposed to assuming baneful magick is at play. Discernment of curses is just as important as knowing how to defend yourself.

However, if your spree of bad luck is going on for too long, there are ways to find out if you are cursed. Ask yourself first if there is someone you have hurt in any way who might want to get back at you. You need to see if there is anyone who wishes you actual harm. Sometimes, these people don't reveal themselves, and part of the curse could be to keep you guessing—siphoning your energy from what is important in your life.

In most cases, curses happen unconsciously—a moment of jealousy from a coworker or the hatred of an ex-lover. These moments place minor curses on you. Deliberate curses typically come from people who have a firm understanding of energy and know how to direct it. If you don't have any enemies or haven't "rocked the boat" of a mage, odds are you aren't cursed.

Nevertheless, let's look at a few ways to see whether or not you are cursed.

There are certain signs you can detect to see if you are cursed. The "symptoms" can be divided into three parts. These symptoms can be found on a psychological, anatomical, or external level.

Psychological Signs

Nightmares – a skilled demonologist knows the quickest way to inflict harm is through the mind. The time when a curse is most effective is when you sleep. Your guard is down, and you can't consciously control your thoughts. A nightmare becomes a powerful means of cursing since it robs you of sleep and messes with your energy throughout the day.

Don't be alarmed if you have nightmares from time to time. However, when the nightmares are persistent with recurring images filled with terror, it could mean you've been cursed. These are typically very specific nightmares revolving around a singular theme.

Depression or oppression – everybody at one point or another becomes depressed or sad. This is the natural way of our emotions: swinging like a pendulum, rising and falling. Ideally, we all strive to find peace somewhere in the middle, cutting off the extremes of these emotional experiences.

However, if there is a heavy-emotional weight that can't be lifted—even after counseling, nutrition adjustment, and relaxation—it could mean there is negative energy at work. It could also mean that an entity of sorts is attached to you. Curses can last for a very long time, and if not treated, they can develop into serious psychosis.

Change of character – when there is a sudden change of character with new unsettling behavioral habits, this development could be influenced by a curse. These new harmful habits cause destructive behavior, which ultimately leads to your ruin.

Feeling of being watched (paranoia) – if someone tries to spy on you, spirits and/or animals can be sent to watch you. If you detect this feeling, even when you are alone, it could be a sign of a curse. However, paranoia can also be a sign of particular mental health issues, and magick should never be substituted for good mental health. If you're constantly feeling paranoia and have consulted with mental health experts, then and then only should you begin to consider curses.

Negative thoughts – when depression sets in, to the point that there is the want to commit suicide, you might also be under a spell. You'll find these dark thoughts lingering in your mind, wondering where they come from. Analyze your mind to see if all the thoughts are yours. Being mindful about your thoughts is key to knowing these things.

Physical Conditions

Some curses focus on harming a person physically.

Headaches – if you are not prone to headaches and there is a sudden persistency of headaches, it could be a curse. Don't confuse it with stress, the odd cold, or any other reason for a headache. Once more, when we're dealing with health, it's important to rule out the mundane reasons first. If there is seemingly "no source" for your headache, then it could be a curse.

Chest pressure – when you lie in bed and feel a pressure on your chest that immobilizes you, it could be an evil spirit oppressing you.

Erectile dysfunction and infertility – these symptoms can be a sign of a curse to a person or sometimes as a side effect of a generational curse.

External Conditions

Some external happenings can also indicate the possibility of a curse.

Immense streak of bad luck – everyone experiences some bad days every now and again. If you are usually a lucky person with things mostly going your way, and there is this sudden string of bad events happening, you could be under a curse. It has to be bad things happening in a sequence over time. Everything that can go wrong, does go wrong.

Just missing out – if you are experiencing situations where you just miss out on getting something, or you keep on just missing an opportunity, you might also be cursed. It is like you just can't get a break. This could indicate something is working against you.

Constant failure in life events – if you are honest with yourself, work hard to achieve your goals, but constantly feel like every opportunity is stolen from you, you could be cursed!

Strange objects – certain practices use broken glass filled with cursed items at the door of the person being cursed to release the hex or spell. If you find this or any other strange object outside your house, it could be done with mal-intent.

Occurrence of animals – sometimes, animals are used in cursing too. If a strange animal appears suddenly and keeps on watching you, it could be an animal familiar sent to bring bad luck or to spy on you. If your own animals get sick suddenly and even die, it could also be a sign of a curse. Dead animals left outside your house are also alarming signs.

Missing items – when a curse is done by a voodoo practitioner, they need something personal from the person. Things like photos, hairbrushes, underwear, keys, or jewelry are items the practitioner would take. Personal items carry a person's DNA, which is often needed for this type of curse. If anything is missing after someone visits you and suddenly your luck changes, you might be the victim of a curse.

Being able to discern is important when it comes to curses. If you're constantly worried you are being cursed, that, too, could be a curse. In fact, the more you try to figure out the who, where, and why behind a curse, the more you strengthen it.

This is why it's important to always seek mundane answers first and resort to magickal conclusions when the mundane has been ruled out. Also, it's recommended to examine your own life and see whether you're perhaps paying a karmic debt of sorts. In most cases, a curse is not likely to be the cause of your mishap.

How to Destroy the Power of Witchcraft

When you start to follow a path in witchcraft, you are bound to encounter negative energy. It's not necessarily that you are looking for trouble, but on this path, you'll be pushing your own boundaries. Perhaps you could have stumbled onto a spell that opened up a negative door in your mind. Perhaps a fellow practitioner becomes envious of your results and begins to send negative energy in your direction.

As you dwindle in the unknown—learning to work with new energies, spirits, and more—you might want to learn ways to protect yourself. It is never bad to be proactive to safeguard yourself or those around you.

When you are unfortunate to be under the power of negative witchcraft, you'll need to learn how to banish or bind the negative energy.

Primarily, your first objective is to rid yourself of the witch-craft directed at you. If you are not powerful enough, get help from a more experienced practitioner. One of the first things to learn is how to banish unwanted energy and negativity.

Banishing Spells

Magick can be an elusive concept when you start to learn more about it. Even for the more experienced practitioner, it could still go very wrong at times. Learning how to defend yourself can go a very long way. There are infinite ways to banish things, and therefore, you'll need to experiment with different techniques that resonate with you.

You "banish" to clear your aura and close down your spell work. A simple banishing spell could be genuine laughter, which completely redirects your attention and energy away from whatever plagues you.

Sometimes, "Laughter is the best medicine!"

Burn It Away

For this, you need paper, a pen, a heat-resistant bowl, and a lighter. Write down what you want to banish and focus on it with a clear mind. Light the paper and drop it into the bowl. As it burns, see whatever is written burn away and disappear. Link your intention with the paper and see how it's being turned to ash. As this happens, burn the image, feeling the sensation in your mind as well.

Some spells involve candles to get rid of whatever is afflicting you. Similarly, you're imbuing intent to the candle, and as it burns, it removes the effects of the curse within as without.

Other Banishing Rituals

There are many banishing rituals you can make part of your arsenal to protect yourself. When there is the slightest notion there is some evil lurking around you, apply one of your banishing rituals to clear your personal aura and free your home from negative energies and hostile spirits.

As mentioned before, every magick practitioner will encounter loads of information to aid their path. Ultimately, the best way to find what resonates with you is to experiment and keep what corresponds with your choice of witchcraft. Hence the importance of your Book of Shadows!

Meditation

To fend off any type of magickal attack, it's vital to keep your head as clear as possible. Control of the mind is absolutely necessary to not fall for paranoia and panic attacks. All negative and unwanted thoughts should be filtered so that awareness of an attack can be successfully warded.

Remember, where your attention rests, energy flows. If you can control your thoughts and learn the art of quieting yourself, you'll be able to banish many curses with no action required.

This is exactly why meditation should be practiced daily in order to gain power over the mental plain.

Protection Magick Is a Must

Protection magick can be seen as a proactive manner of practicing magick. It can be done by making amulets or creating an intentional spiritual or energetic barrier around you, your family, your property, and more.

What makes protection magick difficult is that when nothing happens to you, you know it's working! Nonetheless, it's good practice to create different wards to keep you and your family safe from external attack.

Psychic shield – with a little effort, learning how to do a psychic shield can be very helpful. The moment you succeed in visualizing a protective shield around you and your loved ones, you will breathe easier. You can reinforce this visualization daily, which will strengthen the shield.

Amulets – anything from a piece of jewelry to something made of clay or wood can be used as an amulet. The idea is to inscribe the piece with incantations, runes, or symbols and infuse it with protective energy. Crystals with protective properties work very well as amulets.

In the next part of the book, we will address spells and rituals to banish and eradicate spells.

How to Destroy Unholy Agreements

Very much like curses and hexes, unholy agreements can have a long-lasting effect on your life. Either you enter into an unholy agreement with an entity for a particular gain, or someone else—like a parent—uses you as a bargaining chip in their unholy agreement.

Nonetheless, knowing how to break these agreements requires some additional work.

One of the first steps is to meditate and ask whoever you believe in to show you what the agreement is. It could be your spiritual guide, God, the universe—whoever you believe in. Ask your divine power to open your eyes and ears to gain awareness of what is going on. Earnestly seek a deep revelation to know what you are dealing with.

Once you have divined the nature of the agreement, you can begin to do a "working," which is spell-casting over time.

Steps to Take:

- Every morning and every evening, revoke authority from the agreement.

- Bind any negative energy and spell connected to the agreement.

- Break the agreement verbally.

- Cover yourself with the protection of the universe, or whoever protects you.

- Build a hedge of protection around you that no unwanted entity can penetrate.

- Protect your mind with a protection spell and feed your mind accordingly.

- Repent of anything you did to get into the agreement and atone for that.

- Verbally break any soul tie that linked you to the agreement.

- Pay with a sacrifice (sometimes you need to pay up to unbind yourself).

Use any binding spell you are familiar with to bind the person or entity to hold on to you. A powerful way to cut all ties is to call on Archangel Michael. In a meditative state, call upon Archangel Michael to cut all unholy and unhealthy ties with his sword of flame that doesn't serve your highest good. Ask him to do the same with all unhealthy cords connected to your chakras. When it is done, thank him, and then use healing techniques to restore your energy.

Michael is just one archetype; you can also use Kali, Hecate, Eris, or whichever deity or angelic spirit guide that will best serve your purpose. Just be sure not to come into another unholy agreement to nullify another.

Once again, if you are inexperienced, finding a more experienced witch can be of paramount importance to break these kinds of ties.

2

— . —

Part 2: Preparing for Protection and Reversal Magick Intentionally

As we have already learned, magick works a little differently than institutionalized belief systems. The laws of magick are closer to the laws of physics.

In magick, we believe that:

- **Energy is abundant** – energy vibrates on various wavelengths and manifests as solid matter, liquids, gases, plasma, and more subtle energy fields.

- **Everything connects** – whatever happens on the macrocosm level reflects on the microcosm level. Everything is linked and shared.

- **Infinite possibilities** – magick is not supernatural or miraculous, but if you can imagine it and set your mind to it, it can happen. With belief and dedication, the possibilities are infinite. It's not supernatural—it's just the nature of the universe!

- **The path lies within you** – if you consciously choose something and willfully believe it to happen by embedding it in your subconscious self, it is going to manifest in the outer world.

The heading of this section refers to preparing for intentional magick. To reflect on what intentional magick means, let's take a step back to see why intent is so important.

Without intent, your magick won't work.

You need to form a clear intent and a will to make it happen. However, it is not as easy as it sounds. It might take years to get it right. Many things have to converge all at once.

- You must visualize, clearly and concisely, what you want as if it already happened.

- You must focus on keeping the goal clearly in your mind while performing the ritual that announces your intent to the universe.

- You must induce a strong enough altered state of consciousness so the magickal act can happen on the astral and physical planes simultaneously,

- Your intent has to be filled with passion and direction.

- You must know what you want clearly; if not, you can get something else entirely.

- Know and trust your own motivation well enough to ramp up momentum.

- Believe it will be accomplished.

- Release all negativity in yourself that could prevent it from happening.

- Be in synchrony with the rules of the mundane world or "consensus reality."

Choosing a path of witchcraft and manifesting your desires is very possible, but doing it effectively and consistently takes time. Nothing is just going to fall into place—but don't despair. With a focused mind and consistent dedication, you will get there.

The same can be said about protecting yourself and your loved ones from the results of curses and hexes. This type of protective magick requires dedication, focus, and time to perfect.

Creating a Sacred Space

When reading up on magick and learning about the practice, you have surely come across the reference to sacred spaces. Historically speaking, sacred spaces have always been associated with sorcery and witchcraft. These spaces were typically isolated and very well-protected locations where these practitioners of old harvested the energy needed to do magick with intent. These spaces were where the practitioners focused and used the elements to perform their work.

Today's life is very different—and busier. It is filled with technology and other things that enable people to live less intentionally. It is harder to energetically and physically align ourselves to create magick because of all the noise around us.

This noisiness is why it is good to create a sacred space where you can work without disturbance.

Some practitioners working on more simplistic spells do not bother to create a sacred space for themselves. However, if you want to do more complicated and focused spell work—such as getting rid of negative energy, breaking curses or hexes, or removing negative soul ties—it is undoubtedly a good idea to have a sacred space. A sacred space helps keep you in the right frame of mind, and it keeps unwanted disturbances away. It is a great way to protect yourself while you are spiritually exposed and vulnerable.

There are no set rules in creating a sacred space. Again, it very much depends on the person creating it. Creating a special place is where you establish a connection to the universe. It creates an environment where you can simultaneously feel part of time and space, allowing you to be more focused. A place where you can connect with the sacred, which will make any working feel much more special.

The sacred space becomes your special space where you escape the world, find guidance, and meditate. It is the place where you write in your journal or Book of Shadows. It is the place where you connect to the spiritual world, practice your discipline, and do your magick.

A sacred space is very much a portal to the divine. It is a living expression of your spirituality. From the external world, you connect to the internal world, where you find the truth of your soul.

Where to Put Your Sacred Space

Find a place as far as possible from electric cables, plug points, and chargers. Try not to be too close to generally foot-trafficked areas either. In front of a window, overlooking a garden is a great place. It allows natural light to enter, and it is easier to charge up your magick. But overlooking a garden is not essential, as any natural light will do. In fact, any space can be turned into a sacred space. Some practitioners even use dark rooms and only use candlelight for illumination.

Feel the colors, energies, smells, and how they align with you in a functional and energetic way. It is important to find the correct intention behind everything you are planning to add to your sacred place, as that intention could influence the outcome of your work. Everything within this space has a specific purpose.

Make sure your space is clean—there should be no messiness or clutter. This is because "as within, so without," which means if there is clutter in this space, there is clutter in your mind. This includes dust! (Don't get me started on what dust can do to one's magickal practice.)

The Layout of the Sacred Space

Visualize where the central point of your sacred space will be. From there, you can decide where the four directional points will be located. Symbolic objects can be put on the four directional points to welcome the elemental energies you plan to invoke. For example:

- East or air – feathers or bells

- South or fire – candles or incense

- West or water – a glass of water or seashells

- North or earth – seeds or stones

Make sure you have everything you need at the center point before starting. The moment you start creating the sacred place, you will not want to leave until it is done.

Energizing Your Sacred Space

This is the time when you invite the powers to fill your words with magick.

1. Stand in the middle of the circle. Shake your hands and feet to relax and loosen up the body. Center yourself by taking a few deep breaths. This way, you are getting rid of negative energy and grounding yourself.

2. Visualize a white energy filling your body.

3. The moment you feel warm and tingly, walk to the eastern point of the circle, welcoming the powers of the east and air by stretching out your hand, like greeting old friends. Ask them to fill your words with magick. Typically, we use the left hand to receive energies while using the right hand to direct energies. However, if you are naturally left-handed, the opposite would be true.

4. Turn clockwise to the south, and with the same energy, welcome the powers of the south and fire to ignite your heart with fire. Keep on visualizing the light connecting from the east to the south without

interruption.

5. Move now to the west without breaking the light to welcome the powers of the west and water.

6. Ask these powers to flow into your space with magick.

7. Finally, move to the north by visualizing all points connected now. The connection is now covered all around, above, and below with a white glow. Welcome the powers of the north and ask them to give your magick rich soil in which to grow.

8. Return to the center, and meditate or pray to give the magick time to settle in your mind and heart. This moment is what we call "entering gnosis." Modern equivalents would be "entering the alpha state or the flow state."

9. Once you have entered into a gnostic state, you can then perform your magick with full intent.

10. When you are done, reverse the process by moving counterclockwise and release the powers you called upon. This is known as "banishing," and is very important for the intent to manifest. Banishing can be done in ritualistic fashion, or even doing something completely mundane that removes your attention from your intention. Sporadic laughter is probably one of the most enjoyable banishing rituals there is!

11. Once you have fully cleared out the energies and your

desire to complete your intention, it is time to reflect and jot down whatever you experienced during the process.

The above-mentioned steps are not set in stone. If you find another method that works better, you are welcome to choose it. The important thing is to find the symbolic connection that works for you.

A sacred space is as personal as choosing a path in witchcraft.

The Magickal Mindset

Developing a magickal mindset is, in reality, an awakening. This mindset is where you learn that all emotions can be pivotal in magick, but all thoughts are not. Energy from emotions can be channeled into intent and manifest as a purpose. Thoughts can be more elusive and sabotage your work if you don't take care of them. Thoughts can also be "sticky," so be careful giving too much attention to them if they are not satisfying your soul.

A magickal mindset teaches you how to become aware of your thoughts. It also teaches you how to empower useful thoughts and discard the negativity. When you are in a magickal mindset, all things are possible. Negative mentality can stop you from walking on fire or casting a successful spell. For this reason, you need to retrain your mind. By practicing magick and seeing your spells come true—overcoming obstacles and breaking paradigms—you begin to unlock the magical mind.

Unadulterated Magickal Mind

An unadulterated mind is a mind that has limited social and cultural influences. Think back to the time of the cave people. They saw things for what they were. Childbirth was a miracle. An eclipse was seen as an omen. Wearing certain animal skins for certain powers, vitalities, and strengths of the same animal was an ordinary belief. They saw the world in awe and wonder, and accepted it for what it was.

In our boxed-in way of living, people started to lose that sense of wonder. To practice magick requires a return to that type of mindset. Therefore, you need to reset your mind and take back the right to look at reality with new eyes. You need to understand we are here to learn the magnificent truth of the magickal universe.

It is this unadulterated magickal mind that has brought us specific thoughts, fears, and emotions, which have all kept humans safe. There are perfectly legitimate reasons why we are all born with an innate mistrust or fear of the dark. Some would say this fear has survived through time because humans fear the unknown. However, we do not seem to fear what may be lurking in a fully lit adjoining room. But cloak that room in darkness, and our emotions change completely. We fear darkness because we are, at our core, beings of light. Darkness has, throughout time, represented our enemy. And it is in darkness, it is in the absence of light, it is in the shadows that our spiritual enemies do their work. To break and undo their work, we must bring light, nature, and positivity to the forefront.

Be Responsible

Responsibility goes hand-in-hand with the decision to practice magick. When your values align with your beliefs, you are able to act responsibly. So, ask these questions:

- Why do I want to do magick?

- What do I not do magick for?

- How do I approach magick?

- How do I apply my values and ethics to my magick?

- What am I not willing to do in magick?

Developing a Magickal Mindset

Training your mind to focus on magick takes practice. You need to know clearly where you want to go and what you want to do with it.

Find your inspiration – what about magick excites you? Which of the concepts really hype you up? Is it divination, crystals, or energy work? Do you like herbs, orbs, or black mirrors?

Research and experimentation – building a good foundation is crucial. The more you know, the better it gets. With learning comes experimentation. Do not worry if you don't succeed at first. Practice makes perfect.

Allow yourself to fail – things don't always go as planned. A spell might not manifest as you willed it or fail altogether. Nevertheless, that failure should just be an inspiration to move on and try it again. Modify, adjust, and execute your spells!

Time for magickal thinking – practicing magickal thinking is more important than you may realize. You need to think magickal things for it to become natural. Give your full focus to any activity you can really drill into—like meditation or performing a spell—and believe in your ability.

Use magick at any opportunity – as magickal thinking is getting more natural, start applying it to life around you. See magick in everything and practice how to use it. If you drink a glass of water, bless it and imbue it with magickal intent. Feel the energy in objects around you by hovering your hand over them. Become aware of the subtle energies.

Remain realistic – stay true to reality. Training your mind can open your eyes to other possibilities, but it will do you no favors to lose sight of the bigger picture. Not everything unusual is a magickal sign. Sometimes, something happening around you is just part of life or circumstances. We live in many realities simultaneously, and sometimes, the mundane is just the mundane. Not every bad turn in life is evidence of being cursed—more often than not, it is simply the natural up-and-down rhythm of the universe.

Setting Intentions...Intentionally!

If you look at making potions or collecting material for your practice, it can very much be a mundane thing. If you want magick to work, there has to be intentional intent behind it.

Magick needs strong emotional backing to manifest. It has a lot of mundane parts, but the psychological intent behind the process is what lets magick happen. After all, emotions are but "energy in motion." Magick starts in the mind.

Let's look at this idea from a practical side.

When a practitioner is performing a ritual, they are attempting to impress an idea from the conscious mind into the subconscious mind to allow their subconscious to process that intention. We can call this activity "mental theatrics" since the unconscious doesn't operate in reasonable terms, but rather, metaphors and symbols.

That is the only way for the unconscious to manifest. The conscious impresses on the subconscious to get it to produce a result. It starts with a thought that ends with a physical manifestation of some sort.

How is it different from anything else we do daily? When comparing performing a ritual to the process of making a sandwich, there are not many differences—both are magickal events. You consciously decide to do something and conform that action to your will; the intentions are just not the same. Therefore, when you understand this, you find that magick is happening all the time around us. We are consciously and subconsciously making changes all the time. Knowingly, or unknowingly, we are doing magick in our daily life—continuously.

Our subconscious is always producing results in our day-to-day life.

The difference between a mundane person and a practitioner of magick lies in the intention of the act. Practitioners attempt to have a level of control over the manifestations they desire. For the magickian, it is a deliberate act, and not something that is randomly happening.

Understanding this concept makes it clear that magick can be practiced by everyone.

It is not exclusive and not a gift. It doesn't mean people can't have a natural talent or can't be gifted. But it does mean all these things can be developed with hard work to be produced intentionally. It means that magick is so mundane and built into the very fabric of our minds, we are already doing it without knowing it.

What makes magick work for the practitioner is that it is done intentionally to direct the outcome according to our will. It's not really that mystical; it's part of the fabric of the reality with which we constantly interact. Magick is the mind. The more you work through ritual magick, the more that fact becomes clear. Magick is really one of the underlying mechanics of life, and even the most mundane things are, in fact, magick.

Magick is action, thought, emotion, and anything that can contribute to the subconscious mind where it plays into everything we believe or say that is built on that same fabric. Therefore, this means you don't necessarily have to be a magickian to practice intentional magick; the majority of magick happens unintentionally, after all. But the magickian is aware of what he or she is doing.

So, how do you practice intentional magick?

If you understand that all magick starts in the mind, extensive rituals and magickal tools have a place, but they are not essential. A great magickian performs magick anywhere without needing rituals or tools—only his or her mind. The element of practice is what makes magick so deep that it becomes part of the subconscious. In a way, being a magickian is understanding how intertwined magick is within the fabric of our mind.

With magick being so mundane, is there even a point in doing ritual magick? Ritual magick provides a way to interact with the environment and your life. The tools help your mind make great changes. If you are able to understand your subconscious mind, you can create great changes. It might take years to get to that point, but by developing these skills, you will not just be able to perform great magick, but also be able to get great things done in your life.

The main reason we perform rituals and use trinkets and tools is because our unconscious mind is metaphorical in nature. It doesn't understand "words," but operates in imagery. For example, if I say, "Think of a yellow dragon," you're not going to think of the words "yellow dragon," but conjure up an image of a yellow dragon.

Thus, ritual work and objects become representations of intent, and this way, our unconscious mind can wrap itself around the idea and make it come to fruition. We begin to speak the language of the unconscious mind.

How Do You Set Intentional Intentions?

When you have a dedication like practicing magick, you want your boundaries to be pushed. You want your intentions and desires to line up with your subconscious mind. You want your thoughts to become a reality. To do this, you need to take concrete actions towards making it happen. Just thinking about something will not automatically make it happen; you need to set intentions and execute those intentions to build momentum.

If you learn to set intentions, you will get manifestations.

Remember, intentions and goals are not the same things. Goals can be measured. There's an established timeframe for reaching a goal. Intentions are ongoing with no clear goal to them. An intention becomes a guiding principle for what you want and how to use the energy corresponding to it. Intentions and goals can work separately, but together, they are even more powerful. For instance, a goal has a clear vision of where you want to go, and intentions keep you on your path.

To set an intention, you have to have a very specific goal in your mind. The more specific you are, the better the outcome. The next step is to put action to it to let it manifest. Setting intentions is a conscious act of creation and the first step to get where you want to be. Setting a very clear intention and inviting a certain level of focus on that intention is the only way magick works. Setting a clear intention helps reprogram the thought process to focus primarily on the intention. As a result, you will create patterns and behaviors that bring the manifestation to fulfillment.

Let's use an example: you want to achieve a certain position in your work.

In your mind, you tell yourself that this is going to happen. It is inevitable. You believe it is so. By doing this, you are empowering your thoughts. You are convincing your mind, body, and soul that this can happen. When you do this within the context of a ritual, the ritual is constructed to help you to maintain or get that mindset you need to reach a specific goal. A well-practiced practitioner doesn't always need a ritual as he or she easily can slip into a mindset to set an intention, solidify it, focus intently, and release it. But if you are a beginner and need more skills, a ritual is of great help in setting intentions.

A specifically designed ritual can help reprogram yourself to reach your goal. Magick occurs through the process of intention. If you are focused on a specific outcome, you have a greater potential for it to manifest. Going back to the job aspiration again, setting the intention for getting the job lets you visualize yourself in that position. You are effectively programming yourself by seeing yourself taking command. Consciously, you are thinking of how it feels to have the position and project yourself in that role. You are thinking of the steps to get there. And all this time, your focus intensifies and you build more confidence. And because you have more confidence, you can manifest your goal. This is the exact same process and reasoning we use to clear ourselves of negativity, and break the curses and hexes that may be leveled against us.

So, the work of magick is convincing ourselves that what we want is possible. Setting intentions helps us believe it deep in our core. By deciding an intention will happen, it puts you in a stronger position.

There are many ways to set intentions. But a safe way, if you are starting out, is to do it by using rituals. Rituals are effective because they invite you to a place of receptivity. They allow our minds and sentient state to become receptive to receive messages and tap into our inner power—and the power of the universe.

Bringing it back to practicing magick, setting intentions is most likely the most important part of spell work. After you have created your spell and laid out all that corresponds to the spell, you need to get yourself in the proper mindset. Here are a few ideas for you to get started, and you can do whatever corresponds best to you.

- **Make a cup of tea** – this action helps find the flavor that will best contribute to the intent of your spell. Drink the tea with a mindful intention to help you focus on the energies you are going to work with.

- **Use your Book of Shadows** – write down the clear intention. Do this in your sacred space, or a place where you feel most comfortable and will not be disturbed. Do this for about 15 minutes or so. This is where you drink your tea and start to incorporate the correspondences into your work. The intention can be simple or as complex as you want it to be. Think about where you are right now in your life and what your current level of success looks like. Focus and detail all the experiences you have right now in that area.

Then, think about what happens after the successful manifestation of the spell. Always write that the spell will be successful because any doubt will hinder the process. Write about how your life will be after the spell is completed. Speak as if it has already been completed. Give it power and purpose because that is the whole reason for writing it down. Give it authority to manifest your desires.

- **Relax** – After the intention is set, take a bath to rid your body and mind of all excess stress and energy from the outside world. Before casting a spell, it is important to clear your mind and your body from any negative and unwanted energy from the external. Use purifying salt and herbs to intensify this intent.

Then, go for a walk to balance yourself with the energies of nature. Revive yourself and get in touch with what comes from the universe. Try to clear your mind completely—this is the art of banishing.

- **Meditate** – meditation helps you reach a heightened state of awareness. The purpose of meditation is entering into a deep meditative state where you can achieve an alpha state, or "gnosis." In other words, meditation helps you tap into mindfulness. You learn to accept your emotions, let them go, and declutter the mind. You learn to compartmentalize your thoughts and emotions, and to isolate them so they don't surface during the wrong moments. This outcome of meditation is extremely helpful during spell work, as you only want emotions and thoughts related to the spell to benefit the intent. Single-minded focus is a sign of a great witch!

Meditation helps you reach deeply into yourself and have an increased awareness of the energies around you. This effect will help you stay focused on the task at hand without being distracted.

As you become more proficient in setting your intentions, trust that the universe will lead you to a place of your highest good.

Now that we have a general knowledge base of magick and understand the need for intent, we can explore the specifics of protection magick. So, let's take a look at the tools, amulets, talismans, and objects we can use to protect ourselves, our loved ones, and our property from the negative effects brought to bear by darkness.

Powerful Tools and Ingredients

Symbols, Stones, and Protective Objects to Keep

Warding, shielding, binding, hexing, and cursing are part of protection magick. Protection magick means literally directing psychic energy toward self-preservation or binding those intending to harm you. It is likely the most sought-after power since the beginning of time. With protection magick, you can set boundaries around you, your loved ones, and your properties.

Many techniques and objects can be used to protect a person or property. In ancient times, people looked for protection from harm, illnesses, evil, or accidents. Today, it is still the same. Then and now, people are still asking assorted deities and entities to protect them through special symbols and jewelry to gain protection.

Archeologists have discovered many such charms and objects from ancient times. And they are still found in the modern day. Even the modern Christian churches of today wear such protective charms. Using a cross to declare faith and to be protected by evil is nothing more than a magickal device. It is born from old magick where the priests blessed such objects to protect people against dark magick.

Calling on a spirit or angels to protect you against evil and asking them to set a boundary or protective shield around you is also such a practice. The idea remains the same, and is found in all religions and belief systems. Some symbols and objects are specific to certain gods while others call on a general divine intervention.

How Do They Work?

Many of the charms, symbols, and objects are fundamentally the same, even if their nomenclature differs because of their embedded culture. But a charm or an object without empowerment doesn't really mean anything. Not every necklace is a talisman; not every rock has the power to affect our aura. There has to be an intention behind the charm to work. Charging the energy and vibration of a stone or talisman allows the charm to communicate the intention to the universe.

A protection charm also cannot protect you indefinitely. Meaning, if you put yourself in harm's way—like standing in front of an oncoming car—it won't protect you from the onslaught of the car. Magickal objects and charms ward off harmful energies before they manifest in the physical world. They strengthen your aura and create a barrier or a shield between you and any psychic harm.

Putting protection around you, especially when you are practicing magick, can be practiced daily. It is like putting on a seatbelt when you get into your car to drive. You are not planning to get into an accident, but you're protecting yourself just in case. Your sacred space or work area should always be cleansed by banishing negative energies. A protection shield is like a wall; if you do not clean or banish unwanted energy, that energy stays trapped inside your protective shield.

Protection charms and amulets will help you intuitively become more aware of danger on a physical and psychic level. Think of a time when you felt a sudden urge to change your route back home; your instinct was warning you about a danger you couldn't perceive in this reality. However, within the astral or spiritual realms, your guardian angel or preferred protection method gives you this insight and sends it to your brain through your senses.

Symbols for Protection

Magickal symbols date back as far as 10,000 B.C. They are not related to only one culture, but can be found in all world cultures. Magickal symbols, just like charms, use the energy force of the universe behind them to protect those who believe in them. They act like codes, speaking to the divine mind. As humans, we have difficulty reading and using magickal energy in its raw form, so symbols help the mind process the meaning of the magick evoked.

Symbols also help release the energy to let the magick manifest by separating us from doubt. Using only words allows us to remain attached to our desires rather than letting them go to manifest the act. Using symbols instead helps us perform magick more effectively.

Most symbols for protection are divine symbols based on the manifestation of the sacred geometry of life. They are touchstones of the divine powers, and by using them, we ask the divine powers to protect us. The more a symbol is used with the same intent, the stronger it gets.

• Pentagram

The pentagram is very misunderstood in the Western world. Many relate it to Satanism, but it was created long before any concept of the devil. The five points of the pentagram symbolize the five elements, the five senses, and the form of man. It is a sacred geometrical figure and a sacred protection shield.

In earlier times, the five points were seen as a representation of the five wounds of Christ. But it was also seen as a microcosm or representation of the human being. However, the pentagram is also seen as a gateway to open portals to new energies and spirits, or to banish them. Today, the pentagram is a symbol of modern witchcraft, and many wear it on a ring or a necklace. You could write a whole book on the pentagram alone.

Apart from being a protection symbol, the way you wear the pentagram also has a meaning. If it is worn in an upright manner, it is believed there is a triumph of the spirit over matter and earthly desires. Conversely, it means personal gratification over spirituality.

• Ankh

The ankh is a symbol of life and is of Egyptian origin. It is a powerful symbolic representation of the union of the goddess Isis and her husband/ brother Osiris. Isis and Osiris are the mother and father of Egypt.

In ancient times, the ankh was a mechanism that possessed living characteristics. It meant an ever-living incarnation of God that brings forth blessings and good fortune. In modern days, there are many different interpretations of the symbol of what life means. Some see it as a feminine symbol that represents the womb, where all life comes from. The circle represents eternal life, and the cross below it represents the material plane.

All this, and the name of the "Artist Formerly Known As Prince!" Now that is a deeply rooted symbol!

As far as protection, the ankh protects the wearer from evil forces and decay. It also represents eternal life, and after death, it energizes the spirit to become immortal. It acts as a conduit that connects the wearer to the gods, and so, it presents eternal energy.

- **Cross**

The cross is a very powerful symbol of protection and is used mostly by Christians as a symbol of their faith. Since early times, it was blessed by the church to protect against evil spirits. However, the cross has been around since long before and typically represents balance.

- **Solar Cross**

The Solar Cross is an equal-armed cross that can be surmounted by a circle. It represents the light and movement of the sun for its life-giving energy and predictable cycles of days and seasons. As a protective symbol, it evokes the power of the sun god, or All-Father. It represents both balance and infinity, and is used to banish negativity and cast out shadows.

- **Eye of Horus**

This symbol also derives from ancient Egypt and is now used as a symbol of protection. It relates to Horus, the son of Isis and Osiris. Some also call it the Eye of Ra, but others see Ra as destructive. It symbolizes divine power with an all-seeing eye that protects anything it looks upon. The symbol can also be used for redemption, transformation, and healing.

- **All-Seeing Eye**

This is a symbol of ultimate protection from the goddess. The eye emerges from rays of sunlight. It's also called the eye of providence as it symbolizes the providence of god/goddess protection and intervention.

- **Hexagram**

The hexagram is also known as the Star of David in Judaism, but is found in many other esoteric systems. It has many meanings, like the forces that are meeting above and below in the center. It also represents the four directions above and below, and the four elements. It resonates with the heart chakra and represents unconditional love. This symbol has been used in many different cultures from Judaism to Christianity to Islam. This symbol has six points that act as a protective shield from God for the Jewish people. But for Islam, it represents the ring of Solomon that gives supernatural powers. Hinduism also uses the hexagram to represent harmony and balance between the divine masculine and feminine energy.

Apart from religion, the hexagram is also used in alchemy, where it is used as a symbol for the elements, specifically for balance. Everything points always to perfect balance and harmony in the hexagram, and therefore, many use the hexagram for balanced protection.

• Ogham

The Ogham alphabet is a Celtic symbol system associated with trees. The ancient symbols are used as tools for divination and communication. Certainly, the ogham is used for protection. The symbol L or Luis specifically is used for protection against enchantment and magick. But there are more symbols relating to their corresponding trees that are also used for protection. The ancient Celts used the Ogham alphabet to make amulets for protection.

• Runes

In Norse magick, runes are also used in the form of symbols. They were carved into amulets or talismans, where they were used for protection. The study of runes is very wide, but we can use bind runes as an example. A bind rune is a sigil where one or more runes are combined. They are mostly used for protective charms. The bind rune is set with an intention that would only hold meaning to you. The bind rune can then be worked into an amulet or used in sigil magick.

• Thor's Hammer

Thor's hammer is a Norse symbol associated with the God Thor. Thor is the God of thunder and lightning, and the protector of the commoner. Thor's hammer is extremely powerful and is used for guidance and protection. It's a powerful, unfailing weapon.

• Crossed Spears

This simple symbol has a very direct meaning. Two crossed spears means no entry. Drawings of spears, axes, hammers, and so forth stand for protection. This symbol puts up a psychic barrier to keep the adversary out.

- **Hamsa**

The hand-shaped amulet with an eye in the middle is very popular in Africa and the Middle East. The all-seeing eye wards off bad energy and evil.

- **Zeptogram**

This symbol is also known as the faery star and has seven points (seven is a powerful number in magick). It represents the seven chakras, the seven elements, and the seven days of the week. It is used for protection.

Stones and Crystals for Protection

Stones, crystals, or rocks have been used for many years in a myriad of traditional practices for healing, protection, and attraction. The composition of crystals is astonishing. A crystal has an atomic structure that repeats itself to grow in a specific shape. Six different crystalline families determine the shape of the stone. You find cubic, tetragonal, orthorhombic, monoclinic, triclinic, and hexagonal shapes.

What makes crystals amazing is that they have a predetermined structure that cannot be altered. This quality allows the crystals to form repeatedly in exactly the same way. The defining features of the crystals are formed by these patterns, but this pattern isn't restricted to stones or crystals. Things like sand, sugar, ice, chocolate, metals, DNA, and even liquids have crystalline structures. Every crystal's atomic structure has unique properties that have powerful applications in material science and medicine.

But what does this have to do with witchcraft?

As everything is energy, the strong vibrations found in the stones on a metaphysical level help us strengthen and balance our work. The properties in the stones correspond with the need in us. Crystals, rocks, and stones are used as traditional conduits for magickal intention.

Let's look at some of these wonders of nature!

- **Amber**

Even though we refer to amber as a stone, it is not. Amber is an organic fossilized resin that comes from ancient cone-bearing trees. Some pieces of amber might have plant material or even insects trapped in there for thousands of years already. It has a considerable connection to the earth and is considered a grounding stone for higher energies.

Amber is also a powerful cleanser and reflector of negative energy and disease that can be used to unblock energy. It absorbs negative energy and transmutes it to positive energy. If the negative energy is powerful, amber can literally explode while absorbing it to protect you.

- **Fluorite**

The wonderful rainbow reflections of fluorite make it a beautiful stone for sweeping out negative energy. It is a very honest stone that connects with intuition and shuts off psychic manipulation. As a protective stone, it helps you decipher the truth, and it also blocks geopathic stress. Fluorite comes in different colors that resonate with different chakras. One of the properties of fluorite is making you aware of higher spiritual realities. It links your mind to the universal mind.

- **Hematite**

Hematite brings balance and support to the body. It resonates with the planet Mars, which is the planet of the God of War. This aspect makes hematite a stone of invincibility on all levels—physical, astral, and mental. Hematite can draw out deep-rooted traumas like pulling out weeds. It also protects against geopathic stress and electromagnetic smog.

- **Obsidian**

The obsidian stone is formed from molten lava that cooled down so quickly, there was no time to crystalize. Because of this, obsidian works very fast and with great power. This grounding stone has no boundaries or limitations. Its strong protective properties also render wisdom. Its reflective qualities are unforgiving, as it exposes blockages and weaknesses.

As a grounding stone, obsidian absorbs all negative energy around you. It also has strong healing properties that help unblock negative subconscious and self-defeating patterns. Psychic attacks and negative spiritual influences are effectively warded off and removed. Obsidian is often used in massage to remove negative energy.

- **Jade**

For a long time now, jade has been valued as a protective stone against negative energies and entities. At the same time, it was also considered to enhance creativity and imagination. On a metaphysical level, it has many healing as well as protective properties. It cleanses negativity from your aura and the environment around you.

- **Jasper**

The energy frequencies of jasper are very steady and calming. This stone helps you in times of stress and gives you courage. Jasper also helps a person deal with irrational fears. Many feel that Jasper anchors them in the present and aids with overthinking. As a balancing stone, it clears the mind and protects against negative feelings, moods, and vibrations.

- **Malachite**

Malachite shields against incoming negative energies. It absorbs the pollutants from the atmosphere and protects the body against radiation. The stone also clears electromagnetic pollution and heals the earth's energies. Malachite helps you get to the root of your problems and breaks unwanted behavioral patterns. Malachite is often used to protect against evil spirits. It helps you resolve issues in the past without allowing you to stay stuck in the past. Lastly, it helps you move forward and get rid of toxic feelings.

- **Jet stone**

As another organic stone, a jet stone is formed when pieces of organic material are buried, compacted, and organically degraded. It is then heated and polished to a beautiful stone.

As a stone that gives you physical, emotional, and spiritual guidance, it helps you find balance and accomplish your goals. It can also draw out negative energies that linger in your auric fields. If worn on your person, the jet stone guards against violence or threats.

- **Pyrite**

The shiny component in pyrite often influenced the stone to be called "fool's gold." But the shininess is actually because of iron that forms part of the composition of the stone. "Pyr" means fire in Greek. In ancient times, pyrite was used to create fire by striking it against stones or rocks.

Pyrite shields the wearer against negative energy and environmental pollutants. This stone of action promotes willpower and commitment.

- **Onyx**

Spiritually, onyx is connected to the planet Saturn. Saturn is the planet of Karma, which is the universal law of cause and effect. Whatever energy—good or bad—is put into motion, will come back to you. Because of this, onyx is a good balancing stone. Since ancient times, onyx was worn to ward off negative energies.

As a grounding stone, onyx helps keep your feet connected to the earth. It keeps you protected when the crown chakra is opened to protect you against psychic attacks. If rubbed between the fingers, it helps settle conflicting and strong emotions. This stone absorbs negative energy in your aura and protects your mind.

- **Clear quartz**

The versatility of quartz is astonishing. It is the second most abundant mineral on the planet. Since ancient times, it has been part of the metaphysical world. Crystal clear quartz can amplify energy, which makes it excellent for balancing energy all over the body. When it is used in combination with other stones, it amplifies the energy in the other stones.

Because clear quartz is so adaptive, it can be used with anything and for anything. Many practitioners use clear quartz to amplify other protection stones and their intentions. Apart from banishing negative energy, clear quartz can also release it, which makes it a perfect cleansing stone.

- **Smokey quartz**

Smokey quartz is a grounding and anchoring stone. It powerfully transmutes negative energy by grounding it back to earth. When placed outside houses or in windows, it prevents drifting spirits from entering. Smokey crystals carry the qualities of soil, ash, mud, and clay that help rejuvenate a person.

Its energetic protection property creates an energetic shield around you to protect you from negative energies from others, including dark entities. This quality makes it excellent for protection if you work in toxic environments.

- **Tourmaline**

If you are surrounded by negative people or you struggle with negative thoughts, then tourmaline is for you. You can call black tourmaline stones the etheric vacuum cleaners of yourself and your environment. If you know you are going into a toxic situation, tourmaline will help protect you against psychic vampires and the like.

As a purification stone, tourmaline elevates your consciousness because negative thoughts are internal rather than external.

- **Tourmalated quartz**

This variation of quartz is two crystals in one as it has tourmaline inclusions. Just like other quartz, it absorbs negative energy. Like other quartz, it works on all the chakras, but the tourmaline inclusion allows it to strengthen the third eye and root chakras. This facet makes it a very good balancing stone. Because of its black and white compositions, it is projective and receptive. Clear quartz is a master healer and already a potent stone, so the inclusion of black tourmaline makes it super-powerful as a grounding stone.

- **Turquoise**

Turquoise is likely one of the oldest known stones. As a talisman, it is part of the history of kings, warriors, and healers. It is one of the most spiritual stones in the world of crystals. This stone enhances the communication between the physical and spiritual realm. Releasing rituals often incorporate turquoise to negate the power of old vows or commitments that no longer serve a purpose.

As a purification stone, turquoise cleanses the aura from negative energies and pollutants. Turquoise helps you tap into the protective powers of your spiritual guides. It wards off negative influences and helps you find clarity. Lastly, it strengthens physical and psychic immune systems.

When working with protective stones, it is vitally important to cleanse them before using them. Apart from picking up negative energy, stones also pick up oils, dust, and fats while held in the hands. Remember, a stone vibrates on energy frequencies. It's also important to get rid of lingering energies before you work with stones anew. If a stone is not cleansed, it won't work properly. There are a few ways to do it. Find what best works for you.

Let's look at some forms of cleaning your crystals.

Full moon charging – the full moon releases very strong energy. Cleansing or charging your stones at full moon is delicate yet powerful. Place your crystals where the moon will shine directly on them. Leave them out until about 11 the next morning, as the energy of the sun will strengthen the energy of the moon

Smudging – to clean and recharge your crystals, you can also use the art of smudging. Your preferred dried cleansing herb can be used to filter the smoke over the crystals to purify the vibrations. Smudging often gets used to clear spaces with negative energy. Just remember, working with smoke should be done in well-ventilated spaces.

Water – if clear running water is used, nothing harmful will happen. But some prefer to use salt water to cleanse their crystals. If salt water is your preferred method, educate yourself on stones that don't do great in salt water. Submerge the stones in water and keep them there for 24 hours. Running water also works well, as the movement of the water neutralizes the negative energies hovering around the stone.

Incense – incense works similarly to smudging. The best incense for cleansing is white sage, sandalwood, amber, patchouli, and dragon's blood.

Sound – when you have a large number of crystals that need cleansing, sound can be a great aid. Use an object that resonates with a vibration lasting longer than a few seconds. Singing bowls, tuning forks, bells, and chanting with your own voice are all great methods. Do this for at least ten minutes and allow the sound vibrations to hover over the crystals.

Protective Objects and Other Ways of Protection

There are other ways to protect oneself against negative energy. Some people don't have easy access to stones, for instance, or they might just not be well-informed enough to obtain certain items. The one thing anyone can access without too much effort is herbs. Herbs cannot be discounted for the power they have. Since the earliest of times, herbs have been used by healers and practitioners.

Most herbs have protective properties, so the list of herbs is very long. It's best to study the herbs you are planning to use. Each herb has a special personality and flair that can be partnered with another object. As protection, herbs can be carried in a little pouch, or planted around the house or in pots. It can also be burned when dried or used in teas or potions.

For the purpose of the book, we will address a few herbs, but the possibilities are endless.

Cinnamon – one of the most used herbs in spell-crafting. Cinnamon has very powerful magickal properties. It is used for protection, healing, prosperity, luck, spiritual awareness, and enhancing psychic powers. To protect your house from negative powers, hang a few cinnamon sticks tied together above your door. Smudging with cinnamon also helps dispel negativity and keep the space protected. When you carry cinnamon with you, it protects you from psychic and spiritual attacks.

Dill – the word dill originates from the Norse word "dilla," which means to lull or soothe. In magick, dill is used for money, protection, luck, and lust. It's very effective at keeping away dark forces and for blessing the house. To keep nightmares away, dill seeds are put under the pillow. As an amulet, when worn close to the skin, dill protects against evil spirits and forms a shield around the person wearing it.

Garlic – garlic is another well-known herb that was once worn to protect against the plague. Today, it is still used in many medicinal treatments. For protection, garlic is hung over doors and windows to keep malevolent spirits and vampires out. Its magickal uses also include exorcism, repulsion of psychic vampires, and purification of spaces and objects.

Ginseng – ginseng is another herb that goes back thousands of years. There are numerous benefits of the root, where most are concentrated on general good health and vitality. But it is also associated with protection against negative energies. Carry it with you to protect you against negativity.

Lavender – lavender is known for its calming and soothing properties. Because of its purification properties, it's often used in baths to cleanse negative energies. In modern times, people use it to calm nervousness and anxiety. The plant can be burned to purify your home or workspace. The ashes often are sprinkled around the house to promote calmness and harmony. Dried lavender can also be hung outside the door or in windows to keep negative energy out. During rituals, it is specifically helpful to burn lavender to protect against psychic attacks.

Mandrake – the root of mandrake is small, but packed with magickal properties. Its psychoactive component helps make it one of the world's oldest narcotics. Because its roots resemble the human form, it was often used as a poppet in darker witchcraft. The European version is difficult to acquire, but American mandrake can be found in occult shops. As it is a toxic herb to humans and animals, it has to be dealt with carefully. It can't be consumed or smoked, and the best way to use it is in a talisman or charm. As a protection amulet, it protects the person from possession, and it brings wealth.

Marigold – the Aztecs regarded marigold as a sacred plant. They used it during rituals to guide the spirits to the altars. Marigold flowers can be strung together and hung above the door to ward off evil spirits. It can also be placed under the bed to protect the person while sleeping. Marigold also helps enhance prophetic dreaming, psychic energy, clairvoyance, legal matters. Furthermore, it renews personal energy.

Mint – this is the herb that is most accessible and is very easy to grow. It is well-known for its soothing effect on the body and the spirit. Mint is used to attract wealth and enhance overall well-being as well as protect the wearer. It promotes energy, communication, and vitality. When used in magick, it draws good spirits nearer to aid with the spell or ritual.

In purification, mint's properties are often used in baths to cleanse negative energies and provide a protective shield.

Mugwort – a very popular herb in a witch's pantry because of its strong protective properties. Mugwort grows fast and almost anywhere. It has a bitter taste and antimicrobial properties. There are many different ways to use mugwort, and it was even smoked in olden times as a replacement for expensive tobacco. Modern witchcraft uses it as a visionary herb because it amplifies psychic vision and enhances prophetic dreams.

To protect against bad energy, place mugwort near the door or close to the bed. It can also be incorporated in rituals by burning it over charcoal or using it in smudging.

Oak – oak trees are seen as sacred in certain cultures. Oak bark has been used for medicinal purposes for many years now, as it is good for treating inflammation and pain. Its wood is often used to make magickal tools and its leaves are burned for purification. Both the oak tree and its acorns can be used in magick. As an amulet, its strong protective properties will keep negative and malevolent energy at bay. The smoke of oak helps draw illness out and purifies the air. The ashes of the oak can also be placed around the house for protection against negative energies.

Oregano – this common kitchen herb has already been used for thousands of years. Another name for it is sweet marjoram. Apart from its healing properties, it is also very popular in food. As for protection, when planted around your home, it will keep evil spirits and negative energy away.

Rosemary – since ancient times, rosemary was used in cleansing and purification rituals. It has many uses but for protection; dried rosemary leaves can be left at an entrance to keep evil spirits out. Little sachets of rosemary sprigs can also be put under a pillow to protect against nightmares. Before magickal workings, rosemary can be burned to purify the sacred space from negative energy.

Sage – sage is a well-known herb that often grows in gardens. There are many different types of sage, and not all are edible. White sage is usually used for smudging and is distinct from garden sage, but all sage has magickal properties. Traditionally, it is believed that sage wards off evil, but it is also used for healing. Burning sage will get rid of malevolent forces and negative energies.

Sandalwood – as one of the most expensive woods in the world, sandalwood has a long history of spiritual use in the entire world. For as long as people have been recording history, India has used sandalwood as holy incense. Sandalwood is also used in protection spells and in exorcism. It can be scattered around the house to deter negative energy. It aids very well in manifestation, purification, relaxation, consecration, and peace.

Thistle – thistle is used for protection, exorcism, healing, and breaking hexes. It also cleanses the liver and other organs. It can be consumed as a vegetable, but you can also carry it with you in a little bag to keep hexing spells afar. It can also be used to speed up healing from surgery or illnesses.

Witch hazel – for hundreds of years, Native Americans used witch hazel for medicinal purposes. It is even classified now as a medicinal plant and has FDA approval. Its magickal properties include calling on ancestral spirits, and when used as a talisman, it can call or command intentions. The strong protective properties of witch hazel make it a very popular herb in the practitioner's bag.

Coming to a Conclusion

There is still so much to learn. It's impossible to get into each and every crystal, herb, or amulet to know what to use and what not to use when protecting ourselves against negativity and evil. As you dive deeper into understanding your craft, it would be helpful to make notes. Again, your Book of Shadows will come in very handy here, but I suggest that you have more than one journal. Specific journals for specific information will make it easier to decipher what you want to keep, what you want to archive, and what you want to throw out.

Now that you have gained some information on how to ward off negative energy, I would like to leave you with something to chew on. You have probably created your sacred space by now, and it's most likely in your home. As you sometimes have to leave your home or room, you could pick up negative energy from outside. And even if you have protected yourself, you might sometimes experience a breach. So, what can you do to fortify your protection? Ward yourself against attack!

Putting Your Magickal Wards in Place

Guard your door – put a representation of any magickal symbol or object you like at your front door. When you come to the door, visualize any nasty astral vibes in your aura being cast off and left outside your door. Treat it like a mystical car wash where all negative energy is left behind. Remember to charge the object you leave at your door with the intention to cast off all negativities.

Use a broom/besom — as it is an active tool, by using a besom to sweep just above the ground, all negative energies are swept out. Placing a broom by your front door upside down is an astral "do not disturb" sign. It is a great way to keep unwanted energies, entities, or even unwanted guests outside.

Charm bags — charm bags are very simple to make and you can use them by putting them at all your windows. Put your charm bag together with intention and use protection stones and herbs—or whatever you want—in the charm bag.

Witches burrs — witches burrs can be used in many spells to strengthen them, but they can also be used in your house for protection. You get them from sweet gum trees. They are also easily found at occult stores.

Salt — salt is very easy to use for protection. You can sprinkle a little in all the corners of your house. Just as with all other objects for protection, sprinkle the salt with intention by holding it in your hands for a bit, letting it know you need it for protection. A dash of salt can also be left at your front door to repel negative energy.

Mirrors — enchant any mirror in your home to bounce negative energy back. Mirrors are great objects for magickal protection. Before you use your mirror, wash it with water and vinegar. Then, charge it with your hands by putting them in front of the mirror. In your words, tell it that you want it to be a guardian of the home.

Protective seals – if you are new to witchcraft, protective seals are a wonderful way to start your journey. These seals are completely invisible to the naked eye. You can use oils or infusions made from protective herbs. Use them to draw your symbol—or whatever you want for protection—and seal your windows.

Witch's bottle – take any bottle and fill it up with sharp spiky things. Add something like vinegar or red wine to it; it can be any bottle that you personally fill. Then, put your intention into it. The idea is then to bury the bottle somewhere in your garden or under the porch. This act will ward off any negative energies.

In the next part, we are going to learn about spells and rituals where many of the objects we talked about will be used. Get ready to learn about banishing and eradication spells. It is time to put our knowledge into action.

3

PART 3: SPELLS AND RITUALS

In this part of the book, we are learning more about the essence of spell-crafting. We have already seen in Part 1 what a spell is and that it doesn't differ much from creating a new recipe. What makes it potent is what you put behind it. Remember, a spell is a desire, intent, faith, and energy focused on a particular outcome. There are a few simple principles behind creating an effective spell. But before we look at that, we need to establish the difference between a spell and a ritual.

A seasoned practitioner will know what we're talking about. For a new beginner, all the terms and terminologies can be very overwhelming. Information about the practice, magickal tools, incantations, spells, and rituals are everywhere. So, to rule out confusion, let's look at the differences between spells and rituals. Often, the two words are used interchangeably, but there is a slight difference. To put it simply: all spells are rituals, but not all rituals are spells.

What Are Spells?

The word "spell" is derived from ancient languages where it meant "to signify, to relent, or to talk." It usually has a phrase or a series of phrases with the intention for something to happen. A spell can be cast by itself or happen in magickal practices or rituals.

Spells do not need rhyme, and you can use someone else's spells, too. Writing your own spells is more effective as it comes essentially from you. Remember, magick has to be true. A spell can also be uttered in silence, but it is more powerful when spoken aloud, as words have power. Essentially, spells are the channel to direct energy for a specific outcome.

Spells work like prayers—you ask your version of the source in the universe for guidance and help to deliver your intention. But the difference lies in the physical anchors you use to focus the energy.

Spells can be cast independently of a ritual, but smaller rituals likely form part of a spell. You might meditate before you cast a spell to focus your mind, or you might have a grounding ritual before you start.

What Are Rituals?

Rituals are more elaborate and have more structure to them. It requires more steps like casting a circle and calling on the elements, spirits, or gods. It is something that is repeated in the same sequence of events continually, like the yearly celebration of Christmas.

A ritual often involves a community, like in a church to honor the Sabbath, but can also be performed by yourself. It can be a celebration of something or an initiatory rite. Rituals can include a spell as part of their sequence, but it doesn't need a spell.

Example: It is a full moon, and you focus your attention by meditating on the moon's energy. You read the cards to see what the next cycle will incline. Your crystals are being charged, and you use your journal to write down your intentions for the month. Every month, you repeat this to feel and use the lunar energy, but no spell forms part of it. A spell can be added if there is an additional intention, like finding a job. Then the energy of the moon is channeled to intensify the outcome. So, the ritual included a spell to have a specific result.

Do You Need Tools for a Ritual?

Tools are not absolutely necessary for performing a ritual, but many practitioners find tools helpful in initiating magick. Let's look at some basic tools that can be used:

Asperger – something used to sprinkle water for purification at the beginning of a ritual.

Athame – a black-handled, double-edged, knifelike tool to channel energy. It is not used for cutting. The owner marks it with personal runes and symbols.

Bell – a bell can be used at the beginning of the ritual to alert the four corners and to prepare the practitioner to work in the modes of earth, air, fire, and water.

Boline – witches use this white-handled knife for cutting, carving, or inscribing things during the ritual, like candles, cords, etc. It is usually single-edged, but can also be sickle-shaped

Book of Shadows – the personal magickal journal where spells, invocations, ritual notes, herbal recipes, dreams, divination results, and other material are recorded.

Candles – candles are often used in spells and rituals. The oils they are anointed with and their color have significant symbolic purposes.

Chalice – a goblet for sharing in a ritual.

Charcoal – incense gets often burned on a charcoal briquet.

Cord – this can be either a heavy string used for binding and releasing magick or a cord around the waist of the magickian. The color of the cord often indicates the wearer's degree of attainment.

Incense – you find them in sticks, cones, powders, or resin. The different incense flavor depends on the ritual and energies being invoked.

Lamp of arts – these are the two candles on the altar for illumination. It should preferably be of beeswax, but paraffin will also work. White is the preferred color, but it could also be based on the season or the nature of the magick.

Pen of Art – This pen should only be used for entries into the Book of Shadows or for rituals.

Pentacle – this metal, ceramic, or wooden disc with a pentagram and other symbols inscribed on it is called a pentacle. It represents a symbol of the element earth. Sometimes, salt or cakes are placed on it. In rituals, it can be used as a magickal shield for protection.

Salt bowl – rock salt symbolizes earth. When mixed with water, it is used to purify things by using Asperger.

Sword – a special sword can be used to cast the circle. It is a symbol of air and fire.

Thurible – a metal plate or burner to hold charcoal and incense. It can stand or swing from a chain and is considered an air symbol.

Wand – a stick about 18" carved from one of the sacred woods. It is used to channel power and represent air or fire. It can be decorated by the user.

Water bowl – the bowl is used to mix in salt and is kept on the altar.

There are other tools also depending on the culture and tradition. But these are the basic tools often used by the majority of practitioners.

Creating an Effective Spell

Spells are a little bit like recipes. Everyone can follow a recipe, and everyone can have a manner of success with it. But there are also those recipes that just need a little extra attention for them to be awesome. So, on our journey, we will find many spells that can be useful. But ultimately, we find what works best for us. Remember, we need to be true to ourselves for magick to work effectively. By looking at the following guidelines, you will learn how to create an effective spell.

Spells can be far more effective if some basic principles are used. Let's look at some ideas.

- **Use sympathetic magick** – in magick, we always look for correspondences because like attracts like. Positive thinking will attract positive results. If you are casting a spell for protection, look for pointy herbs and thorns corresponding to psychic protection. Find something that connects to the purpose of your spell, and if you understand the connections, it will function well.

The most effective spells are those that have a direct connection. This is why in traditional folk magick, they often make use of parts of a person's body, such as fingernails, hair, sweat, urine, or blood. The DNA of such items has a stronger energetic connection. But so can a blessing to holy water add the same intention to ordinary water when added to the water.

Bell's Theorem explains it well. It says that any object once in contact with another continues to affect each other when separated by distance.

- **Maintain the balance** – it is all about balance. Think of the yin-yang symbol—each side has a part of the other, and both flow into one another and exist in perfect balance. When things are out of balance, it always creates chaos and disruption. Nature shows it to us time and again. For us, it lies mostly in our emotions. For instance, men get taught that it is weak to embrace their softer feminine qualities. It brings discomfort to demonstrate vulnerability. But to be a fulfilled human being, accepting that man has part of woman, and vice-versa will let him or her operate in perfect harmony.

When we practice magick, we also have to maintain a balance of the forces in our work. Maintaining a balance of all four elements is the desired outcome but try at least to keep two opposites balanced. When you invoke air, call on earth, too.

- **Use all five senses** – the more senses you use, the more effective the result. If all five senses are put together to work on the same purpose, the subconscious mind understands it more clearly.

- **Don't over complicate** – simplicity is the keyword here. The more complicated you are, the more confused your subconscious will be. Use things you understand easily and practice them until you can do them without thinking. If you wake up in the middle of the night, you should be able to perform the spell.

- **Give back** – energy is neither created nor destroyed. That is a law of physics. In quantum physics, we learn that energy seemingly coming from nowhere is borrowed from the future. Whatever you take from the universe has to be returned. How you do it is entirely up to you. You could thank the Source of Creation with gratitude, or you can make an offering to the universe. You could transmute one elemental force into another. Find a way to give back; if not, your spell could be weakened or not work at all.

- **Magickal symbolism** – our subconscious mind works well with symbolism. It recognizes and functions faster when personal symbolism is used. Group symbolism is where several people decide on the meaning of a symbol and give it a semblance of consciousness. In magick, this means an egregor. Deities are in effect egregores because they are the personification of a large group of people. These people mutually agreed on the specific traits they have. So, when you connect to one of these deities, you connect to all the energies related to them.

There are many egregors found in religions, nations, covens, and social clubs. Our minds understand them easily. Invoking an existing egregor into your spells allows magick to follow a less resistant path to travel. A well-known egregor in protection magick for banishing is the pentagram.

- **Trust the universe** – if you do something half-heartedly, it is doomed to fail. The preparation for spell work is essential. Remember, setting intentions and following through on them will only work if your mind is set accordingly. Do whatever you need to do to rule out any negativity and contradictory thoughts. When in doubt, do not proceed until all doubt is ruled out.

Potential Hazards When Magick Is Misused

Magick should never be used to harm innocent people or with anger and vengeance in mind. Even well-intentioned magick can be harmful without the permission of the person involved. You could interfere with whatever that person has to learn. Ethical magickians will only perform rituals and spells for others if they are asked and only if it's proper and wise.

But what could go wrong if it wasn't mindful enough? What disturbances might occur when messing with spell-crafting?

- **Energy Imbalance** – a practitioner's body channels a lot of energy and power during a spell or ritual. Grounding the excess of energy is important because, if it is drawn from its own power, the practitioner will be left with no reserves and be exposed and vulnerable.

- **Excessive introversion** – when you are too involved in the astral planes, it is possible to neglect the Earth-plane affairs. You should never neglect your family, job, or earthly activities. There always has to be a balance.

- **Temptation leads to corruption** – the more powerful you get, the bigger the temptation. It would be easy to use magick out of fear, anger, or greed. Listen to your inner voice. When in doubt, ask someone you know who is ethically strong to guide you.

- **Non-material interference** – when we use magick, it draws the attention and presence of other creatures from other planes. The magickal circle operates on both astral and real levels. When energy is released, it acts as a beacon and alerts the attention of these entities. There are basically three kinds of non-material entities that could interfere. These are not deities—they are elemental spirits, non-human life forms, and discarnate humans. Most of them aren't harmful, just curious and will disappear when losing interest. They are only harmful when there is a weak or damaged energy field due to substance abuse or trauma. They can also bring harm if the practitioner is mentally confused or on certain incapacitating drugs. Be careful not to leave your body open by allowing your spirit to leave if you are not well-protected. This point emphasizes the importance of a clear mindset again. The best way to counter any harmful effect is to work in a well-protected circle.

- **Wrongful successes** – if you don't understand your deep karmic needs and you focus on superficial conscious goals, you are setting up false success trails. You will save a lot of energy if you focus your goal in harmony with your true will. Listen to your subconscious mind until your conscious mind understands.

Remember, whenever you venture on the path of learning to cast spells and practicing rituals, take it slowly and carefully, and listen to your common sense. Stay grounded, centered, and balanced. Your goals must be worthy of magick.

"For magick to be successful, emotion must push a link outward into the magickal universe; imagination must aim it towards the desired goal and feeling must affirm the reality of which is sought." - Unknown

Now, how do we learn to protect ourselves?

Banishing and Eradication Spells

Now we are coming to the part where you encounter banishing and eradication spells. First, let us look at the difference between banishing and eradication.

Banishing – in ceremonial magick, banishing has to do with removing non-physical influences like spirits or negative energy. It is almost always done by performing ritual magick. The ritual can be complex or it can be simple. Ceremonial set-up is not a requirement, and can therefore be done by an individual.

We have also established that to clean the workspace of a practicing witch, a banishing ritual should form part of a daily routine. As a transitive verb, "banish" means to drive out or remove from a place of usual resort.

Banishing rituals for daily practices are short and focus on grounding and centering you. As mentioned, it also keeps negative forces out that otherwise would try to derail the spell you are working on. One of the most famous banishing rituals is taught by the Hermetic Order of the Golden Dawn and is called the Lesser Banishing Ritual of the Pentagram. There are many other banishing rituals you can look up in your own research that would work just as well.

Eradicate – this means to destroy and remove utterly.

Banishing spells should be done with great care. They require deep meditation and should only be done to people who cause intentional or unintentional harm. But don't be afraid to banish someone from your life if they are destructive and disruptive.

The spells that follow are a compilation of spells found from different sources. Even though they work and can be used with confidence, you are more than welcome to write your own.

Spells to Destroy the Power of Negative/Harmful Witchcraft

Protection and Banishing Spell 1

This is a powerful protection spell against people out there to harm you.

You will need:

- Coarse sea salt

- Five tea candles

- One black taper candle

- Candleholder

Create a salt pentagram – the pentagram forms the foundation of the spell. The four cardinal directions, plus the spirit, resemble unity. This powerful symbol displays all the energy of the universe and contains all essential elements for life.

Use the salt to draw a pentagram on a flat surface and put the five tea candles on each point.

Charge the tea candles – do this with your unique intention. Use an individual candle at a time and hold it in your hand. Focus on the intention of the spell. Breathe the intention down onto the candle to infuse your will into it. Place each candle back on the points and invite each element of each direction to help you.

Charge the black candle – with the black candle in your hands, begin infusing it with the powerful intention of protection against harmful persons or negative witchcraft. Do this until you feel it is complete. Place it in the middle of the pentagram.

Create an energy dome – dig deep into the strong emotions and intentions of protection. Start creating a dome of energy that infuses your candles and salt. Light the candles and visualize the dome extending over and around you.

Speak an incantation – as you are surrounded with protective energy, say the following:

"Banish the harmful and all the bad

Keep out the anger and the sad

Ancestors, Angels, and Spirit guides

Guard me through my daily strides

Against all ill thoughts, hex, and curse

A protective shield shall disperse

As I do will it, so mote it be!"

Protection and Banishing Spell 2

This is a banishing spell in its most basic form. By visualizing, this spell focuses on the harmful person or harmful energy against you. No additional objects are needed.

Step 1 – close your eyes and visualize a circle of light around you. Breathe in deeply and fill the circle with your awareness.

Step 2 – breathe out all the air in your lungs while imagining how the circle is shrinking as you let go of your awareness. Continue for 1 minute by expanding and contracting the circle.

Step 3 – focus on the negative witchcraft or energy you want to banish. Feel and visualize the negative energy, and fill your circle with it as you breathe in.

Step 4 – firmly and intentionally, breathe out and visualize how the negative energy is expelled and sent away.

Step 5 – repeat step 4 until you are certain it is gone. It will feel lighter every time.

Step 6 – finally, cut the air with your finger or a wand to dismiss the circle.

To banish something, you need to bring it closer first. Then, you need to become aware of its presence. You need to clearly know what it is and how it feels. In essence, you must accept that it's here, and then let it go by banishing it, never to come back.

Protection and Binding Spell 3

Binding negative energy and witchcraft are powerful. Just as with banishing, the aim is to keep harmful witchcraft at bay.

You will need:

- A pair of scissors

- A pen

- Black thread

- A small discrete photo of the person you want to bind. The photo has to be as current as possible as the focus is on present actions. The photo also has to be filter-free with no other attachments added. Make sure that no other people or animals are included in the picture.

Attention! This work requires dedication and energy. You have to be sure you want to bind the actions of the person. Your intention, will, and energy must agree with the ultimate goal.

Step 1 – take the photo in your hand, and with mindful energy, look at the photo and focus all your strong emotions about the harmful actions of the person on the image of the person.

Speak to the person as if he or she is standing right there and call the name out.

Tell the person that all the horrible and harmful things he has done has to stop. Explain with strong emotions expressing your anger, frustration, and feelings why you want them to stop. This will create a link between your emotions and the image in the photo.

Repeat this step of expressing your feelings and stating why you want the harmful actions to stop until you feel it settles.

Step 2 – flip the photo over. Write the complete name and date of birth of the person at the very top of the picture. If you don't have all the information, write as much as you can. Doing this will link the photo to the actual person.

Step 3 – under the name, write what it is you want to stop in or from that person. Also, write why you want it to stop and why you want to bind these actions. As you write this, focus all your frustration and anger on the person. You have to feel the anger and disdain of what this person has done, either to you or someone else. The more force you put into the pen, the better.

Step 4 – turn the picture 90 degrees counterclockwise. Sign your own name once, or three times, across the photo with all the energy you can muster. You are now signing your purposeful energy with conviction that it is going to work.

Step 5 – fold the photo in half and feel the desire and frustration for this negative energy to stop. Your intention and desire have to roll into the picture for this to happen.

Step 6 – turn the folded photo lengthwise and roll it away from you. This indicates getting rid of something. Take the black thread and loop it over the edge. Start binding it tightly while focusing on the action of binding the harmful actions. Do this by repeating the name and date of birth of the person. Also, repeat what it is you want to bind and why. Don't lose your intention and energy while doing this. Act as if the thread represents you and the petition, and the photo represents the negative actions of the person you are binding. Take control of the situation and keep on speaking into the situation until everything is covered.

Step 7 – loop the thread over your finger and pass the photo object through to form a knot. You are welcome to use knot magick, where 9 knots are used. With each knot, express why you are binding the person. Then with a strong voice say something like, "I bind your actions against me and every negative thing that you have done." When you feel that you have completed the task, cut the thread. Your work is done. Keep it in a safe place that represents removing or trashing things. The darker the place, the better.

If the binding over time loosens, you can repeat the binding by tightening more black thread over it again. To get rid of the binding, throw it in a fire.

Spells to Break, Destroy, and Rid Negative Hexes, Curses, and Spells

Breaking curses depends very much on the type of curse. If there is physical evidence, like magickal remnants of an object, it is easier to break the curse. If you find such an object, use uncrossing oil, and draw a personal sigil or a sigil of a friendly spirit over the cursed symbol. This way, the cursed symbol becomes your own, and you destroy the curse.

If you find objects like an amulet, bottle, or jar, simply break the object. The curse will also be broken. But some spells also can be exercised to break a hex or a spell.

Breaking and Destroying a Curse Spell 1

This simple spell can be used without much practice. Follow the steps conscientiously and carefully.

You will need: □

- The person or item that was cursed (yourself, if it was you).

- A large enough tub to submerge and wash the target.

- Enough sea salt to make the water-to-salt ratio 100/1. If you use a lot of water, it is better to use too much than too little salt.

This particular spell is best performed during a new moon, on a Thursday at noon or at midnight. It can also happen at dusk or dawn, as long as it's a time of transition.

Step 1 – fill the tub with water. If it's a living thing, the water should be comfortable.

Step 2 – open the salt container and hold it over the water

Step 3 – clear your mind, and say the following with intention and confidence: "In the name of my ancestors, my gods, and myself, I call upon thee, oh creatures of Earth and Water. Come forth, cleanse (name of object or person) of evil and alien magicks, and restore (them, me, it) to balance and health. By our wills combined, so mote it be."

Step 4 – pour the salt into the water.

Step 5 – remain in a meditative and focused state while submerging the target slowly. If you are the target, lay back and soak in a relaxed state.

Step 6 – stay submerged for at least 10 minutes. When you are done, drain the water and rinse it off the target. All salt water has to be washed off.

Step 7 – finish the ritual by saying the following in the same mindset as step 3: "I thank thee, oh creatures of Earth and Water, in the name of myself, my gods, and my ancestors.

Be released to your homes, doing no harm on your way, and return to me with glad hearts when next you are summoned. By our wills combined, so mote it be."

Uncrossing Spell to Get Rid of Curses and Hexes Spell 2

"Uncrossing" literally means to get rid of something unwanted. If you suspect you are hexed or cursed, an uncrossing ritual could set you free.

You will need:☐

- 1 handful of bay leaves as protective herbs

- Cinnamon powder for purification

- Two frankincense incense sticks as the uncrossing agent.

- 1 white candle

- 1 dish

- Lighter or matches

Step 1 – visualize a protective circle and take three deep breaths to empty your thoughts.

Step 2 – light the white candle on your altar.

Step 3 – place the bay leaves in the dish.

Step 4 – as you sprinkle the cinnamon on top, say this: "In the name of the victorious elements, I invoke the ancient forces. To crush and remove all negative entities, all curses, and crosses. Break and dissolve. Bless and set free. As it is now, so mote it be."

Step 5 – cross the two incense sticks on the dish and light them.

Step 6 – let the candle and incense burn out completely.

Spells to Break, Destroy, and Rid Unholy Agreements

Similar to getting rid of curses and hexes, there are many ways to get rid of unholy agreements. We have established in Part 1 that an agreement or an oath is willfully made between two parties, at the least. This agreement can be made between two or more human beings. It can also be a solemn promise made to a God, another spiritual entity, a king, or something else.

Sometimes, agreements made in past lives still bind you subconsciously. It has an effect on your present living conditions. For instance, you are divorced, but don't feel free. It could be that you had an agreement made in a past life not to divorce, but it was broken, and guilt is now attached to it. The divorce might be the right thing now, but the guilt from the broken oath in the past unconsciously affects you now.

Then there are past life covenants that are legally binding agreements that now have misaligned effects. One sign of such an agreement is when you constantly get into trouble with the law. Another sign could be fear of legal contracts. Any irrational fear or behavior could be symptoms of remnants of past life covenants affecting us today.

Dissolving Unholy Agreement Spell 1

You will need:❑

- Paper and a pen

- Candle

- Matches or lighter

- A tranquil place to meditate

Step 1 – find a place to be quiet and prepare your mind. For this exercise, the subconscious mind needs to place you in an altered meditative state. Focus your intent on getting to an unconditional mind with positive expectations.

Step 2 – decide on what type of ceremony you would like to break the agreement. You could write a decree where you solemnly decide to break the agreement. State why you are breaking the covenant.

In this meditative state of mind, ask:

- Is there any way this agreement benefits my life?

- Does it interfere or harm my life or others?

- Can I resolve the issue, or do I have to get rid of it?

Step 3 – write a request to nullify the agreement in the name of the Spirit you prefer. Focus all intention on the written decree and see it vanish before your eyes. Fold the paper and burn it over the candle.

Step 4 – scatter the ash in the wind or bury it.

Breaking an Unholy Agreement Spell 2

You will need:

• Writing paper

• Pen

Step 1 – identify the contract you are under.

Step 2 – set your mind to clearly become conscious of the power of the agreement. Write out everything that comes to mind. Writing in detail how the agreement affects you and controls you is the first step in breaking it. This might take some time or even a few tries, but you must list all the possible ways the agreement affects your life.

Step 3 – go into observation mode. Observe the behavior and the power of the agreement. Consciously put distance between you and the power of the agreement. Note what relationship dynamics activate your awareness of the power of the agreement. Observe how and why you became vulnerable to the agreement, and how you fell under the control of the other person or entity involved.

Step 4 – on the notepad, ask how your life will change if you break the agreement. Look at all the facets around the agreement. Then, select one agreement interaction and consciously create an opposing behavior. If you need approval, sense how you feel when you are ignored and how your world spins out of control. Exaggerate the feeling of rejection and dread. Shift instantly to the opposite direction, where you feel completely in control of your life and in no need of the other person or entity.

Say the following prayer: "I am detaching myself from the agreement and I am breathing my energies back into my wholeness. I am choosing not to be under the control of this agreement. I will not negotiate my spirit to or for this individual." Consciously withdraw from the influence of the contract. Open your eyes, and know that you are fine and in control. You are now liberated from the power of the agreement.

Step 5 – believe you are set free. Be aware not to fall for a power play. The other part knows your vulnerabilities and would try to gain them back. Don't give in to any susceptibility to the agreement. You will know when you are victorious because you will immediately sense psychic freedom.

Spells to Reverse Hexes and Curses Back to Sender

By using protective amulets or having strong guardians, you most likely will never notice a curse or hex cast upon you. It would bounce off and go back to the sender. But there might be times that an obsessive attacker will not let go and hit you on all levels. This is when you use reversal magick to let the attacker fall into his or her own trap.

Go through the usual steps of identifying the attacker or finding strange objects around your living area. Remember, you need to be sure you know who it is. This is why you always do divination before you reverse a spell and send it back to the cursor. If it's not the right person, the curse will be sent back upon you. Use your preferred method of divination to establish the source.

Reverse Hexes and Curses Back to Sender Spell 1

Upside-Down Candle Reversal Spell

You will need:

- Black candle

- Candleholder

- Pot of dirt

- Powdered crab shells

Step 1 – mentally tap into the frequency of the powers set against you. Light the black candle and put it in a candle holder. Concentrate with an intention on the candle so it represents the original curse.

Step 2 – the moment your mind grasps the power of the curse, pull the candle up from the holder and snuff it out in the pot with dirt and powdered crab shells. Crab shells are not necessary, but it strengthens the spell because crabs walk backward.

Focus with the intent of reversing the curse upon the sender. Take the candle and bite off the bottom of the candle, revealing the wick.

Step 3 – light the candle at the bitten end and place it back in the holder. While doing this, say: "Thy Artifice has been reversed; Thy Curse has been returned. By Force and Fire and Cunning Will; be thou the victim of thine own ill."

All must be done in an emotional state of justified anger, especially the snuffing out and biting part.

Step 4 – let the candle burn all the way down. Gather the wax and the dirt, and either deposit it at your enemy's house or throw it into moving water.

Mirror Box Reversal Spell 2

You will need:

- A small tin – the smaller, the better (a small wooden box or cardboard will also work)

- A small, new mirror to fit the tin.

- Glue

- Black candle

Step 1 – clean the box very well to stick the mirror into it. The mirror should ideally fit most of the box.

Step 2 – fit the mirror into the box. If you cannot find one that fits perfectly, you can use a few smaller ones or broken pieces. At this point, don't look into the mirror because you don't want your energy trapped in the box. If you accidentally saw your reflection, burn sage to purify the mirror by passing it through the smoke.

Step 3 – glue the mirror onto the inside of the lid of the box. Hold the mirror until it sticks. Prevent looking into the mirror by covering it with a black cloth.

Step 4 – put a representation of the person who cursed you inside the box. If you don't know the person, use a small doll or piece of paper that says "The Hexer." Place the item in the box facing the mirror.

Step 5 – close the box and put a black candle on top. Seal the box properly.

Step 6 – when the candle is firmly set and the box is sealed, say a spell or prayer asking for the curse to be reversed. Send the curse back to the sender. You could say: "Sender of evil, menacing foe, after this spell you reap what you sow. This mirror reflects the will that you send, my hands are clean, my spirit will mend. With this spell, my soul is free. As I will, so mote it be."

Step 7 – light the candle and let it burn out.

Spells for Jinx Removal

A jinx is very close to being cursed or hexed. The difference lies in that a specific object in your possession might cause harm. Jinxes are also seen as bad luck following a person around. If you suspect you are jinxed, the first step is to put up protection spells that can block the effects. Identify any object you suspect could be intending the harm and get rid of it. Then do a cleansing spell.

How to Remove a Jinx Spell 1

You will need:

- 1 green candle

- Cinnamon powder

- Salt

Step 1 – place the green candle on your altar.

Step 2 – spread the salt in a protective circle around the candle while saying: "Bad Luck, I command you to leave me right now."

Step 3 – light the green candle and say: "All adversity now dissolves."

Step 4 – focus, meditate and visualize all the problems going away.

Step 5 – after 5 minutes or so, sprinkle the cinnamon on top of the salt and say: "Only good luck and positive energy now flows to me."

Step 6 – visualize all the good energy and luck coming to you like a bright light. See all the positive things manifesting in your life. Cancel all negative thoughts and energies, and replace them with new images of success and good fortune.

Step 7 – let the entire candle burn out.

Remove a Jinx in Your House Spell 2

You will need:

- 6 votive candles

- 1 black candle

- A pinch of rosemary, black pepper, and cinnamon.

- Fireproof bowl

- Hot charcoal

- Matches

- White ceremonial sage incense stick

Step 1 – place the 6 white candles in a circle.

Step 2 – get into the circle with the mixture of cinnamon, black pepper, and rosemary.

Step 3 – light the 6 white candles with a match. Then light the black candle with one of the white candles.

Step 4 – meditate and focus on the harmful jinx with the intention to remove it from you and your house. Visualize how it's leaving you.

Step 5 – when you feel confident the jinx is leaving, say: "Whatever evil comes to me, I cast you back. I have no fear. With the speed of wind and dark of night, may all your harboring take flight. With the swiftness of the sea and all the power in me, as I will, so mote it be."

In a loud voice say: "I cast you out!" Then, blow out the black candle as hard as you can.

Step 6 – you can either remain in the circle, repeating the words "I cast you out" until the white candles are burnt out, or you can stand up and blow out the white candles.

Step 7 – light the sage incense stick and walk through your home. Be sure to fill each room with the smoke of the sage. Cover your hands and body also with the smoke.

Step 8 – after the candle wax, charcoal, and white sage have cooled down, place it in a white cloth. Tie it together and bury the white cloth in your backyard.

Spells to Destroy and Rid Negative/Evil Energy

When there is a strong sense of evil energy lingering, it could very well be that dark magick is involved. Most of the time, the intent behind the person practicing dark magick is to harm someone out of revenge. The free will of the person can be replaced by the caster's will to manipulate the person. Dark magick uses the evil magickal powers and supernatural entities to satisfy their evil acts with the intent to harm a person emotionally, physically, or mentally.

Evil energy can be placed in a person's house or the attack can be direct. If you hear or see anything strange happening around you, you might be under attack. Look for these signs:

- Unexplained knocking on windows or doors

- Unexplained lights

- Hearing unknown voices in the house that you can't

find

- Stuff in the house move by itself

- Doors and gates open by themselves

- Objects and pictures fall down without reason

- Lights turn on and off by themselves

- Objects disappear from the house

Spell to Banish Evil Energy: Spell 1

You will need: □

- 1 red apple

- 1 bay leaf (fresh or dry)

- Knife

Step 1 – place the apple on your altar or a table in front of you. Focus with an intention on the apple, sending all negative energy away. Rid all evil energy.

Step 2 – with mindful energy, visualize a protective shield around you that bounces all negative and evil energy off.

Step 3 – cut the apple in two and put them on the table facing up.

Step 4 – put the bay leaf on top of one of the halves. Say: "Red and Green, Banishing Grace. Cast all evil out of this place."

Repeat this 3 times with a loud voice. Believe in your subconscious mind that it is happening. Meditate with intent until you feel it happens. A deep level of faith is necessary.

Step 5 – when you are convinced it is done, take the two halves and put them back together. Bury them in fresh soil.

The Olive Oil Ritual to Remove Evil Energy: Spell 2

You will need: ☐

- Olive oil

- Plate or bowl

- Pair of scissors to cut the shapes formed by the oil

- Salt and water☐

Step 1 – pour one drop of water onto the plate or bowl

Step 2 – pour 3 drops of olive oil into the water. If the oil forms a circle, the evil was done by a man. If it forms an elongated shape, the presence of evil was caused by a woman. If the oil spreads evenly all over, there is no evil energy and no harm against you.

Step 3 – if it indicates evil, chant or say a prayer by calling on your preferred god or gods to get rid of the evil. At the same time, cut the shapes formed by the oil with the scissors. Don't stop until you feel the evil energy gone. All the circles should disappear.

Step 4 — use salt and water to clean your house to get rid of any lingering evil energy. You can also put salt in the corners of every room to keep negative energy out.

Spells to Destroy and Rid Negative Entities and Demons

Demons are different from ghosts because they can attach to humans, animals, or homes. Ghosts are mostly spirits who don't yet realize they have passed on. Demonic influence is always more intense and violent. Demons can even attack you sexually or take control of your mind. Sometimes, a rotten smell lingers to indicate there is a demonic presence. Several evil entities can cause all sorts of grief. In some cases, you might need professional help, especially when possession is imminent.

Often, the energies at work are low-level spirits, servitors, djinns, or trickster spirits attached to you to mentally break you down. If you suspect demonic intervention, try to pinpoint what could have attracted it. Then, do a cleansing ritual and a protection spell to protect you and your loved ones.

Removal of Demonic and Negative Energies: Spell 1

You will need:

- Broom

- Iron nails

- Oil burner

- Music

- Oils – cedarwood oil for purification; banishing oil; myrrh oil for protection

- Herbs for warding off evil spirits like mullein, St. John's Wort, or nettle

- Incense like frankincense or agrimony to expel negative energies

- Cedar smudge stick

Step 1 – begin by sweeping out every room in the house, starting at the furthest back. While you do so, put on music with a frequency that helps disrupt the energy patterns of the negative entities involved (search on YouTube for some music if you don't have any). When every corner is swept and all clutter is removed, put bowls with salt in all the corners for protection.

Step 2 – enter your sacred space and form a protective shield around you. Get into a meditative state and focus on all the negative energies and entities around you. Drop cedarwood oil on the burner. While the oil burns, visualize how the oil is creating a barrier between you and the negative energies. You can also dab the oil on key areas of importance to you.

Step 3 – when you feel confident that the demonic presence has left, turn the burner down. Light any one of the incense sticks to protect you from and expel any lingering spirit and negative influences. Say a prayer to the deity of your choice. Psalm 23 is a popular choice, or you can say: "My house is cleansed, my home is clear. Only good spirits may enter here."

Step 4 – walk through the house with the cedar smudge stick and fill every room with smoke to protect and get rid of all demonic influences.

Step 5 – use iron nails to protect your premises by driving them into the grass or trees outside. You can also hang an iron horseshoe upside down at your front door to keep demonic spirits out.

Expelling Demonic and Negative Energies: Spell 2

You will need:

- White sage for smudging

- Lighter

Step 1 – open all the doors and windows to allow the spirits to leave. Light the sage and let it burn for 30 seconds before you blow the flame out. Allow the smoldering sage to cleanse the space of negative energies by moving it in all the corners.

Step 2 – chant a prayer or a mantra to chase the demonic influences out. Psalm 23 is popular, but it could be any prayer or mantra you have. Keep repeating it. You can say something like: "No demons are welcome in this space. I command you to leave. This is a place of light and love."

Step 3 – use music to disrupt the negative energies or use pots and pans by banging on them. Walk through the house and repeat the mantra again.

Step 4 – place salt in the corners or use holy water and the like.

Step 5 – if you have done everything and still detect a presence, call in professional help.

Spell to Destroy and Rid Bad Habits

You will need: ☐

- Black candle

- Pen and paper

Step 1 – write down the bad habit you want to get rid of on a piece of paper.

Step 2 – light the candle and stare into the flame as you clear your mind of all negative thoughts.

Step 3 – burn the paper in the flame of the candle while chanting: "With this cleansing flame, I banish you from my life. So, mote it be."

Step 4 – formulate a new intent by writing it down on a piece of paper. The new intent must be positive. Some examples:

- To stop smoking: "I'm a healthy non-smoker."

- To stop procrastinating: "I feel motivated to get things done."

- To stop biting your nails: "My nails are healthy and strong."

Step 5 – for the next 21 days, write your new intent down 3 times on a fresh piece of paper.

Spells to Destroy and Rid Psychic Attacks

As mentioned before, psychic attacks are very much like curses. The only difference is that the one attacking you doesn't necessarily use tools or ritual magick; they simply use their mind to willfully cause harm, pain, or misfortune to a person. Another form of psychic attack is mesmerism where a form of mind control that suppresses the will is practiced. In many cases, these forms of attacks are unintentional or the practitioners just don't believe it's a form of magick. They rather see themselves as persuasive or good talkers.

Triangle of Defense Technique to Rid Psychic Attacks: Spell 1

You will need: ☐

- Your sacred space or a place where you are not disturbed

Step 1 – close your eyes and start turning slowly in a clockwise circle. With intention, feel the direction from where the attack comes. You should feel a buzzing either in your third eye or solar plexus. You could also feel it in your heart or hands.

Step 2 – stand your ground and face it head-on. Visualize a cobalt-blue or violet light pentagram at your third eye.

Step 3 – bring your hands up to your third eye, palms facing out and thumbs and first fingers touching. It creates a triangle in front of your forehead. This is called the Triangle of Manifestation used in spell work to consecrate tools and charms, but here, it is used to manifest your will for protection.

Step 4 – step forward and project your hands forward, sending the triangle to the source of harm. With intention, sever the link and shield yourself from further attacks.

Step 5 – this step is optional. The process can be sealed with the Lesser Banishing Ritual of the Pentagram. But cleansing and banishing rituals where banishing pentagrams face all directions will also seal.

Candle Spell Against Psychic Attack: Spell 2

You will need: ☐

- Your sacred space or altar

- 3 candles

- Matches or lighter

- Full moon

Step 1 – enter your sacred space and calm your thoughts by meditating. Light the candles.

Step 2 – imagine a blue energy ball forming above all 3 candles.

Step 3 – caress the candles and say:

"Goddess of Three (you can use the Deity you work with), I call upon Thee.

To protect me from those who wish to harm me.

Keep them from using the gift from Thee.

Keep them from using thy gift to harm me."

Step 4 – see how the blue ball explodes into blue lines. Imagine the blue lines surrounding you and wrapping you in blue energy. See how the blue light forms an unbreakable shield. Acknowledge the protection of the deity you follow.

Step 5 – let the candles burn out by sending all their energy into your shield.

Cleansing and Manifesting Rituals

Cleansing Rituals

Cleansing is one of the most important parts of practicing anything spiritual. The purpose of cleansing is to remove any unwanted and negative energy. It's specifically cardinal before doing a work of any kind. You don't want any unwanted energies influencing a specific spell or ritual. Everything should be cleansed from your workplace to your tools.

Don't forget yourself because unwanted energies can also cling to you. It's like clearing a garden from weeds. Any negative thinking and turbulent emotions we allow take root very quickly. With meditation and prayer, we can reseed our consciousness with healthy thoughts, feelings, and impulses. It's vital to take time out to tend to the soil of your psyche. The process of letting go and letting in allows your conscious to agree with your highest desires.

Negative thoughts and emotions will definitely affect your cleansing rituals if you don't get rid of them. It will block your creativity and intuition. If you are not sure how to do this, here is an example that could help. Repeat this prayer before you start cleaning your workplace:

▫Dear Powers of Goodness,

▫Allow the sweet sound of a quiet mind to soothe my aching heart.

▫Allow any disease in my body or darkness in my thoughts

▫To spontaneously transform into nectar for my soul.

▫Allow my anger, sadness, discontent, vanity, envy, jealousy, and grief.

▫To dissolve instantly and rebirth as spiritual nourishment.

▫Allow the force of my intention to permeate my experience

▫And reflect back to me the sweet nature of my deeper heart.

▫Let the voice of the divine return me to my holiness.

▫Today, I choose to shower myself with your grace and your blessings.

▫Today, I choose to reclaim my holiness

▫And be an inspiring expression of yours.

▫You are my beloved, and my beloved is me.

▫And together with you, I say, "And so it is, and it is so."

When you have taken care of yourself, you start by actually cleaning your house and workspace. Cluttered spaces do not promote positive energy for spiritual workings. When your living area is clean, continue by cleansing the area of negative energies.

The most common cleansing method is smoke cleansing by using bundles of dried herbs with cleansing and protective properties. Instead of dried herbs, incense can also be used. Walk with a lit incense stick through all the rooms and fill the space with smoke. Incense with protective properties includes frankincense, dragon's blood, rosemary, and sandalwood. There are many more you can choose from. Bear in mind that sage removes all energy, both positive and negative. So, you want to burn something after you use sage to bring positive energy back. Rosemary and lavender work very well for that.

When fire or smoke is out of the question, you can use sprays to cleanse the areas. All the different incense flavors are also found in sprays. Just as with smoke, walk around the area and spray in all the corners to remove the negative energies.

Sound is also a way to cleanse the area. You can use wind chimes, sound bowls, or bells. You can also use music with a positive vibe to push negative energy away. Put the music on when you physically clean the place to simultaneously push out negative energy.

Your tools and crystals also need cleansing. Crystals are a bit more specific, and you need to study up on how to clean them properly. It is very important to cleanse your tools after you just bought them as you don't want unwanted energy to enter your workspace. You can use smoke or running water to cleanse the tools.

Burying crystals underground is also a way to cleanse them. It can also be put on a bed of salt or rice as both are good for absorbing negative energy. Leave it overnight and it should be good to use.

The moonlight is also good to cleanse your crystals and working tools. The sun can also be used, but it should not be left too long as some crystals can lose their color.

Selenite is also a great way to cleanse your tools. Use a slab of selenite to lay your working tools on.

Spiritual cleansing baths are excellent to cleanse yourself.

Visualization is another way to cleanse your space and yourself, but it is a bit harder. You have to use your own energy to cleanse your tools and not lose concentration. So, other methods might be easier.

How often you decide to do a deep cleanse depends on your own working methods. It's advisable to clean your sacred space every time before a working.

Cleansing Ritual: A Pre-Spell Spiritual Bath: Spell 1

Cleansing and purifying baths are used to get rid of negative energy and the influences of evil spirits. It is often necessary to perform a ritual bath before casting spells. Spiritual baths provide an extra layer of protection when we feel vulnerable. They help strengthen our spiritual defense barriers.

You will need:❑

- Rue

- Bay leaf

- Rosemary

- 1 white candle

Step 1 – add 1 teaspoon of each dried herb to a pot of water. Bring to a boil and let it simmer for 20 minutes.

Step 2 – while it is simmering, take a regular bath or shower to clean yourself. Prepare the bath by lighting a candle and putting on some relaxing music.

Step 3 – when you are done, take out the filtered herbal water and pour it over you. Start from your head and work your way down. During this process, clear your mind and relax.

Step 4 – if possible, air-dry yourself rather than use a towel.

Herbal Aura Cleansing Ritual: Spell 2

If you are feeling tired or you have no strength, this cleansing ritual is the right thing. This ritual helps deal with anxiety, depression, and spiritual blockages. It helps renew the spirit and attract positive things. This bath can be taken any day of the week, but is more effective when taken with the new moon to start the lunar cycle with a clean aura.

You will need:

- 1 sprig of rue

- 1 sprig of rosemary

- 3 leaves of Guinea hen weed

- 1 white candle

Step 1 – fill up the bathtub with water to your liking.

Step 2 – light the candle and put relaxing music on (the music is optional)□

Step 3 – add the herbs to the water and mix well.

Step 4 – soak in the bath for at least 20 minutes or more. □

Step 5 – air-dry if possible; if not, use a clean towel.

Cleansing Ritual for Your Home: Spell 3

You will need:

- 1 lemon

- Salt

- 4 cloves with the heads still on them

- 1 glass bowl

Step 1 – rinse the lemon to clean it of all unwanted energy. Then, with intention, awaken the protection energy of the lemon by setting the needs of protection. Feel the energy awaken.

Step 2 – cleanse the glass bowl.

Step 3 – use a knife to carve your name into the lemon. Cut the lemon in half. Put one half into the glass plate.

Step 4 – hold the cloves in your hand and cover them with your other hand. Charge the cloves by speaking your intention into them. Place the four cloves in the four directions onto the lemon. This placement is to protect you all around.

Step 5 – take the salt and charge it with the intention to protect your home and everything within it. Put the salt around the lemon in a circle. The amount of salt is up to you.

Step 6 – leave the bowl in a secure place in the room you want to protect. It should preferably be in the middle where no one can touch it. Leave it there until the lemon dries out.

Step 7 – when the lemon is completely dried out, the negative energy is absorbed. Cast the lemon in the trash. This way, all negative energy gets taken out with the trash.

Deliverance Spells

Deliverance is nothing else than being set free from whatever is oppressing you. It's when you are taken out of the kingdom of darkness and transferred to the kingdom of light. Deliverance is breaking the hold the oppressor has on you. When you come to understand the tactics and strategies of the oppressor, you can break free.

The following simple ritual is to put the past behind you and to be totally set free. This basic ritual can be adjusted to fit any possible thing you want to be set free from.

Deliverance Ritual: Spell 1

You will need:□

- Meaningful pen

- Paper

- Fireproof dish

- 3 white candles□

Step 1 – place the candles in a triangle with the tip facing away from you.

Step 2 – light the candles. Focus on the candles with mindful intention and say, "I will undo the past tonight so that the future might be bright." Repeat this with all three candles.

Step 3 – write down everything you want to be delivered from. (This can include abusive behavior against you, or what you inflicted; an addiction that won't let go; unfaithful behavior, etc.) Write a short description on its own piece of paper. Be brutally honest!

Step 4 – take 3 deep breaths and say, "I accept what I did do, now I move forward to the new." Burn the first written piece of paper. Repeat the phrase with each piece you are burning until only the ash remains in the bowl.

Step 5 – stand up and say, "The future is here, I am on my way. This is my will, this is my say. The new has begun, my will shall be done."

Step 6 – extinguish the candles, take the ashes outside, and let the wind blow them away.

Step 7 – relax or sleep. It is done. □

If the oppression you are suffering from is more serious than just behavioral issues, you might want to do a deliverance ritual in which a sincere invoking of a higher spirit is needed. It is vitally important that your relationship with the Higher Spirit is long-established and strong. If you feel you can't do this alone, find a group of experienced people to help you.

Ritual for Deliverance of Spiritual Oppression: Spell 2

You will need: ☐

- Your sacred space or a calm environment

- Candle of your choice

- Lavender incense

Step 1 – invite your spiritual guardians to protect you on all levels. You can light a candle of your color that you feel connects you to them. If you are not sure, choose black. Meditate until their presence is felt.

Step 2 – affirm your faith in the Higher Spirit and the belief that you will be set free in the power of the Higher Spirit. That by the power of the Higher Spirit, all the power of the universe will be released for you.

Step 3 – lay down all pride, as pride blocks the path for deliverance. Express your total need for the Higher Spirit to deliver you from the oppressing entities. Open yourself for deliverance.

Step 4 – confess your involvement by letting these spirits in. Ask forgiveness for letting your guard down or for practicing negative things. Let your subconscious mind show you un-righteous deeds done by you. Be brutally honest.

Step 5 – repent for all unrighteous actions with a truthful heart.

Step 6 – forgive those who acted unrighteously against you. There should be no dark thoughts in your heart against those who mean you harm. Forgiveness is a decision and not an emotion.

Step 7 – break from all harmful practices. Remove any object that might have negative energy and connection to unwanted intruders.

Step 8 – be free from any curse over you.

Step 9 – confirm your stand with the Higher Spirit. Believe that he stands with you. If you hear a name of a spirit, act on it by saying, "You, Spirit of Rejection (example), I take my stand against you in the Name of the High Spirit (or the Deity of your choice). I only submit to the higher power. You have no place in me. I command you to go!"

Step 10 – pray the following: "Oh Divine High Spirit, I believe that you are in control of all things in the universe. I humble myself before you. I put aside all my pride and dignity, and I confess all harmful activities and hold nothing from you. I break all connections to unwanted spirits and entities. I am free of all curses over me. On this ground, I ask you to set me free and deliver me to receive the deliverance I need."

Step 11 – in a loud voice say, "I speak to all spirits. You are already defeated in the name of the Higher Spirit. In the name of (High Spirit), I command you to go!"

Step 12 – give thanks to your Higher Spirit. It creates an atmosphere that oppressing spirits don't like.

Step 13 – release your spiritual guardians.

Step 14 – when you feel it is done, protect yourself with a protection shield. Stay protected by all means. Protect your house and belongings, too.

Manifesting Fruits

"For a good tree doesn't bear bad fruit, nor does a bad tree bear good fruit." - Luke 6:43

After all we have been studying so far, there is always the concern of keeping up the good work. What if you are cursed and it affects your practice or your person so much that you are laid lame? How can you keep on through oppression with your head still high and producing good fruits

We have learned how to do protection spells and rituals for warding off harmful energy. We also understand the importance of practicing rituals and using all sorts of magickal tools. But what stands out most is your own spirit. If you don't learn how to use the defensive techniques of the spirit, you are not running on all power. We are part of the Great Spirit, and through the power of spirit, all things are connected.

So, apart from learning to do reversal magick and protection, you can also learn to defend your spirit. What's in the heart defines a great spiritual warrior. The compassion you have for other living things starts within yourself. Remember, we are all connected. Even if you would send harmful energy away, it never disappears. It just remains locked away. In our aspiration for a perfect balance, we should rather strive to heal. If we can overcome our ego, we can find the alignment again to bring back harmony.

So How Do You Do That?

Prevention is better than a cure. Before you react to a situation, reflect on it. Meditate to find the higher purpose for the conflict in your life. Are you supposed to learn something? Are you teaching someone else something? Understanding brings new fruit upfront.

Bless your friends and foes. When someone attacks you, it often comes from disharmony in them. They're out of balance. When you bless them instead, they tend to get so busy with their own good fortune that they forget about you. Wish them all the best for the higher good. Remember the law of attraction? Send out blessings, and blessings will be bestowed on you.

Laugh a lot and be joyful. Diffuse serious obstacles by laughing at them. There is magick in laughter. Laugh all your problems away, or at least give it a good go! When you are too serious, you put your energy on defense. That energy also converts easily to fear, and fear breaks down confidence and power. It makes you weak and leads to energetic blocks and illnesses.

Fear allows fearful energies to feed off your fear and makes them stronger. Laughter and joy let them turn away sometimes without even banishing them. Laughter from the heart is full of joy and love. Both are a great manifestation of good fruits.

So, for you to bless someone else is, in essence, a blessing to yourself. By blessing someone, you are asking for divine favor and protection. The power of the universe allows the person who is blessed to live in harmony. It changes the negativity around the person to one of gratitude.

The same goes for casting a spell of happiness onto someone or yourself. It has long been proven that laughter is the best medicine on many occasions. Before we go on to the next part where we will learn how to protect ourselves, we will look into a blessing and a happiness spell.

Blessing Spell for Manifesting Fruits: Spell 1

You will need: □

- 1 white candle (or a figural one in the gender of the person you want to bless)

- Blessing oil of holy oil

- Photo of the person

- Piece of paper and a pen

- Saucer or little plate□□

Step 1 – carve the person's full name on the candle.□

Step 2 – dress the entire candle with a blessing or holy oil.

Step 3 – write the name of the person on the back of the photo or on a piece of paper.

Step 4 – place the piece of paper or photo under an over-turned saucer. Let the candle stand on top of it.

Step 5 – for seven days, burn a portion of the candle every day. Light the candle and say:

"(Name) be blessed

May all good things come to you

May nothing whatsoever harm you

May your heart be light

May your travels be safe

May your health be good

May your mind be sound

May your friendships sustain you

May you be blessed in every way"

(Any special request you have to the person can also be added)

Step 6 – snuff out the candle by pinching the wick between your fingers.

You can continue with the blessing spell as long as the person needs it.

The next spell is a spell to cast happiness. This can be directed to someone, but it can also be for yourself. Modern medicine is a great help today and important in managing certain conditions. But nature's medicine fortifies our healing process. Nature heals and helps us combat fear, anxiety, and depression.

Happiness Spell for Manifesting Fruits: Spell 2

You will need: ☐

- A picture of the person

- 1 royal blue candle

Step 1 – place the picture of the person down and put the royal blue candle in front of the picture.

Step 2 – close your eyes and focus on the person in the picture. Imagine the person laughing and being happy. Think of total contentment in life and happiness in friendships and relationships. See this happening in your mind's eye.

Step 3 – open your eyes and stare at the candle. Be sure to see the picture of the person behind the candle, too.

Step 4 – with fixed intention, say:

"Happiness and glee,

Make their anger flee.

Long-lasting and forever,

Make their happiness ever so clever.

This spell will last.

Make their happiness come up fast."

It's always better to meditate before this spell is cast. To secure the spell, it also helps to cast a circle before casting the spell.

Protection Spells

Feeling emotionally and spiritually unsafe can put a strain on your overall health. It can also drain you of all your energy. Apart from protecting yourself against negative onslaughts, it will also help you find stability in this stressful world.

Just as with any other spell, protection spells need focus and intent to affect change. You are the agent of change where you form and direct energy towards the desired outcome.

For protection and defense magick, you need a specific set of intentions to help you cleanse and cast out negativity. You also need to cleanse your space and any tools you are planning to use. Remember to always express gratitude when the spell is done.

Protection Spell for Deliverance from Destructive Habits

This spell is best to be performed in the last days of the moon cycle.

You will need:☐

- 1 black candle

- 1 white candle

- Paper

- Pen

Step 1 – place the white candle in the middle of your altar. Set the black candle next to it, facing the nearest window.

Step 2 – write down the outcome of what you want to be manifested. State it as done, "I am free of my addiction to cocaine.

Step 3 – tear the paper into 7, 9, 11, or 13 pieces. The number depends on the severity of the addiction. Place the crumpled pieces of paper next to the black candle in a row facing West or to an open window.

Step 4 – Light both candles. Meditate and visualize the desired outcome. See and feel how you are set free. Take the paper nearest to the black candle and set it alight. Then move the black candle one space away from the white candle. Blow the candles out.

Step 5 – According to the number of times the paper was torn, continue in the same way as described in step 3. Every night, the black candle moves one more step away from the white candle.

Step 6 – When everything is burnt to ashes, take all the remaining wax and ashes and dispose of them. You can either bury it all or let it drift away in running water.

Step 7 – Use the moon as a reminder that your addiction is broken. It might run the full cycle of the moon before you are totally set free.

Protection Spell for Body and Health

You will need: ☐

- 1 white candle representing purity and divinity

- Something sharp

- Your intention□□□□

Step 1 – Clean your sacred space and the tools you are going to use to rid them of negative energy.

Step 2 – Meditate with the intention to be protected. Focus on everything you need to be protected.

Step 3 – Carve into the white candle your intention, like "I am protected from harmful energies." Be specific about what you want to be protected from.

Step 4 – Spend some time with the candle. Put your thoughts and intention into the candle. Meditate for as long as it takes to feel the satisfaction that you are protected.

Step 5 – Light the candle with the same mindset and intention. Look into the flame and see a white protective light surrounding your entire body. Take as long as you need to feel the protective energy from the candle.

Step 6 – While keeping your intention and meditating, let the candle burn out.

A Spell for Your House and Home

You will need:

- Bells

- Light blue candles

- A pen

- Matches

- 1 candle of your choice

- Sprig of rosemary

- Rosemary essential oil

- Piece of rose quartz (tumbled stone size)

Step 1 – cast the spell the day before traveling or on a Wednesday. Take the pen and write the astrological symbol for Jupiter on the candle (Jupiter is the planet that rules travel).

Step 2 – take the candle in your hand and visualize what the purpose of the candle is. Focus on how it is used for protection while traveling. Take as long as you must to get a clear visualization of protection. Think of all the facets of your trip and where protection is needed.

Step 3 – put a few drops of rosemary oil on the candle. Put the candle in a fireproof holder and light it. Place the rosemary sprig on the top of the candle and the rose quartz in front of the candle.

Step 4 – gaze into the flame of the candle and say, "By the light of the lady moon, I will reach my destination soon. The trip shall be safe and happy for all concerned, as well as me." Repeat this incantation 3 times. The Jupiter symbol has to melt into the wax and rosemary oil.

Step 5 – snuff the candle out. Rub some of the rosemary oil onto the rose quartz while projecting safe travels.

Protection Spell for Health

<u>**You will need:**</u>⬜

- Sweet grass

- Piece of aloe vera for healing power

- Pieces of white sage as antibacterial

- Lavender for comfort

- Dried rose petals for protection and beauty

- White quartz to absorb all negative energy

- (Add anything you think can contribute to healing in the jar)

Step 1 – start by adding smoke of the sweet grass in the jar to remove any negative energy.

Step 2 – add the other ingredients one by one, meditating on the healing and protective properties they have.

Step 3 – top it off with anything that could bring color to the bottle to inspire healing.

Step 4 – seal the bottle with wax to keep all the good energy inside. Speak your intention for healing over it.

<u>Protection Spell for Your Business Success</u>

The best time to cast this spell is during a waxing moon until the full moon. The best days to do it are on Sundays or Thursdays☐

You will need:

- Golden candle

- Dark green candle

- Patchouli oil

- Orange oil

Step 1 – prepare your altar or workplace. Cleanse all your tools and the area you are working in.

Step 2 – use both oils to cover the candles. First, start from the middle of each candle and spread the oil upwards. Then, move the oils downwards, starting at the middle again.

Step 3 – place the dark green candle on the left and the golden candle on the right of your altar.

Step 4 – light the dark green candle first, then the golden one. Meditate, and with intention, visualize prosperity and success for your business. Clearly see a prosperous and successful business.

Step 5 – stay in the meditative state while feeling success and prosperity on all levels. While the candles burn down, feel your energy and the candles energies intertwine. Bask in the utmost feeling of success.

Spell to Protect Animals and Pets

For this spell, we will use brown candles because they relate to Earth magick. They invoke grounding, stability, and nurturing. We also use the prayer card of Saint Francis, but if you feel uncomfortable with praying, you can use the Strength Tarot card instead.□

You will need:

- 1 brown candle

- Glass of water

- Photo of your pet

- Saint Francis prayer card

- Strength Tarot card (Optional)

Step 1 – prepare your altar with a cleansing ritual. Place the brown candle and the glass of water a few inches apart on the altar.

Step 2 – place the photo of your pet between the candle and the water. If you don't have a photo, write your pet's name on a piece of paper.

Step 3 – hold the payer or Tarot card in your hand. Focus your intention on the card and say, "Protect my pet, my beloved companion. And I promise to take care of my animal as you take care of yours. If my friend is lost, let them come back to me. Bring me joy and strength, so mote it be."

Step 4 – sprinkle a few drops of water on the photo.

Step 5 – let the candle burn for a few minutes, then blow it out.

Step 6 – cut out the burnt tip of the candle and bury it along with the photo somewhere on your property. It can also be buried in a pot plant.

Step 7 – throw the water away and give thanks to your prayer card or Tarot card. Put it back in its place.

Protection Spell for Your Winnings▢

You will need:

- Rice

- A bowl

- Coins

Step 1 – prepare your altar by cleansing it to get rid of negative energy.

Step 2 – place the bowl, rice, and coins on the altar.

Step 3 – prepare your mindset by meditating.

Step 4 – put one coin in the bowl and cover it with some rice. Repeat the sequence until all the coins are covered with rice. The last coin can be exposed.

Step 5 – speak your intention into the bowl. Visualize abundance and constant flow of your gains.

Step 6 – put the bowl somewhere hidden in a corner of your house or business to invite prosperity from all four corners of the universe. It will also be protected from negative energy.

This brings us to the end of Part 3. I hope this part was an enlightening experience to strengthen your journey. Incorporating spells and rituals into your practice requires diligence and a great portion of faith. Willingness to experiment can lead to disaster or success. But how you handle it is what counts.

In Part 4, we are going to look into how to maintain victory and deliverance.

4

———.———

PART 4: MAINTAINING VICTORY

You will soon discover that once you get a grip on all the information and knowledge shared with you in the previous parts, the actual work starts. You will understand and accept that spells and ritual work do not automatically free you from possible obstacles. You must embrace the truth that the end is the beginning, and the beginning is the end. As the universe itself is infinite, so is your process of awakening and mastering your craft. Therefore, there is no need to rush without building a strong foundation. Once you have rid yourself of hexes, curses, and dark agreements, you're free to go as far as the imagination permits.

It doesn't matter if you accumulate all of the knowledge in the world; if you don't apply these methods and get real results, how would you know what works and what does not? You will have to figure it out for yourself. Magick is about getting what you want by exerting your will onto the universe and utilizing your internal belief systems to manifest new realities. It's about coming into flow with the core elements of the universe—tinkering and influencing your surroundings while simultaneously shaping your internal world.

People tend to think that when you practice protection and reversal magick, you will be safe from all dangers. Life would simply be easier. However, when it comes to exerting your will on the Universe, you'll have to overcome many challenges, some within and some without. One could argue that the more you begin to grow within your power, the greater your challenges will become.

However, this is not a bad thing!

On the contrary, greater challenges are heralds of growth. It means you are on the right path, moving closer to your soul purpose.

This is what many mystics refer to as "The Great Work," which is endless! It requires commitment, dedication, and consistency to scale up your magick. And when you are faced with adversaries, your spells will be swift and effective.

Maintaining a healthy spiritual, physical, and environmental balance in life seems simple, but it can also be profoundly complex. Working within the paradigm of magick brings change. How we handle that is up to us. There will be changes made to our mind and our spirit that ultimately can influence our health, wealth, emotions, and much more! The longer we operate within the magickal paradigm, the more we are exposed to the complexity of how power, life, and our role within the manifesting world all converge together. This path takes a lifetime to walk, and the more we walk, the more we realize how little we know.

Nonetheless, the biggest issue with protection magick is that the way you know it is effective is if "nothing happens." Rather, nothing adverse happens to you. Of course, this book is about ridding yourself of hexes and curses. Once you have achieved your goal, the objective should be to inoculate yourself against psychic attacks of any kind.

When you are effectively holding up your wards, you are mastering your protection spells. The instances of "bad things" should diminish to the point where they almost become non-existent. This, unlike other spells in magick, requires the absence of "bad luck or ill moments" to illustrate its effectiveness.

Therefore, as you continue with this last portion of the book, we'll be taking a closer look at different methods to maintain your protection and inoculation from dark magicks. However, it's important to understand that just like your own immune system, your spiritual immune system can be vulnerable at times. Sometimes, a rogue curse or hex might pass your defenses; this is okay. With the knowledge presented in this book, you will have the right response from now on. You now know how to rid yourself of dark magick.

You have the magickal arsenal of the aforementioned chapters to rid you of any non-resourceful thought, action, behavior, attitude, person, etc. from your life.

Let's Refresh Our Knowledge of What a Curse Really Is

We have already in-depth discussed the difference between hexes and curses in Part 1 of the book. We have learned that it is truly harmful and can even be inherited. The intention behind a curse or a hex will always come from a negative point of view. The purpose is, without a doubt, to bring harm and even destruction.

We also discovered that though curses or hexes could be intentional, it's also very possible to unintentionally curse someone or even yourself. Out of anger or frustration, you can lash out at someone. The lashing out could be coupled with heavy-hitting words directed at the identity of the other person. Sometimes, unburdening yourself from these dark thoughts can be refreshing, and other times, you can still taste the bitterness of the act after the fact. This is the simplicity of a curse: it simply requires intent, emotional frequency, and a target.

Or you can also curse yourself with negative thoughts and attitudes. Something as simple as saying, "This year will never end on a high note." Or, that you never have money and will always be poor. You are cursing yourself on a major scale, creating limiting beliefs and imprisoning yourself within your own mind.

If you are intentionally cursing someone, you have to envision the curse in your mind. This means you have to authentically feel the hatred and pain you desire on the person. You would have to wholeheartedly and honestly desire that person's destruction. By creating this image in your mind, you are, in effect, cursing yourself. This is because in order to curse someone, you have to conjure up an image of the person within the imagination, which would then forever be framed as the "cursed version of your target." The problem being that the image you conjure is not your enemy, but yourself, wearing the mask of your enemy. In simpler terms, an image of someone else in your mind can only exist if you hold it in place. As cursing is a deliberate action, it can't be taken lightly. There is always a price to pay. That is why deliberate curses are not so common. Any experienced practitioner understands that the energy it takes to curse someone and to sustain its effects has a blowback on the caster, so practitioners tend to find other ways to achieve their goals. It has been said that if a caster needs to resort to hexing someone, it only shows their inability to manifest their desired realities. They have to focus on "someone else" as opposed to building their own universe according to their will.

Nonetheless, if you are experiencing bad luck all the time and nothing ever goes right, then it's good to explore the reason behind it. Just remember that no one's road is just filled with beautiful fragrances and sunshine. Tribulation is part of our lives. Some bad times and moments are there for us to grow. In other words, your bad luck might simply be part of your journey of growth. Ultimately, before you arrive at any conclusion, you have to analyze your situation.

Are You Really Cursed, Or Is It in Your Mind?

You always have to start first by looking at all the general reasons why things are not working for you. Sometimes, it is as simple as changing an attitude or behavior to turn things around. Sometimes, it's not even a curse, but rather something within your energetic field that needs to be dealt with. This is why it's always important to first check in with yourself before you jump to any conclusions. Meditation and mindfulness become powerful allies to help you identify when things are coming from you or are directed towards you.

If you dive deep and still cannot find any obvious reasons, then a curse may be a culprit. Even so, it still doesn't mean that you are cursed by someone specifically. There could be various other reasons for your spur of bad luck. Sometimes, you are facing a life lesson, and instead of trying to "dispel" the bad luck, you're supposed to lean into it and learn from it. As mentioned earlier, our lives are not about sailing through it painlessly and void of problems or conflict. Discomfort is the hallmark of growth, and those who embrace it go on to achieve great things. In relation to curses, they can come from an external or an internal source. Just remember, your mind is a powerful thing and if you instruct it to look for curses in your life, it will find them! Fortunately, the opposite is also true: if you direct your awareness to find blessings in your life, it will!

Internal and External Cursing 101

What do I mean by this statement? How can a curse be external and/or internal? Nothing is ever just black and white. In the book, we looked at all the different kinds of curses. We also saw there is usually a great cost attached to performing curses. Nonetheless, this doesn't mean there isn't something else trying to negatively impact your life. They may consciously or unconsciously become a detrimental force in your life. To better understand the concept of internal and external curses, let's quickly take a look at how they differ.

What Do External Curses Mean?

When someone deliberately puts a curse on you, it's seen as an external action; it did not come from within you. A person has taken time to contemplate and construct ways to harm you. All of this intention directed towards you is destructive. When you are externally cursed, you have no part in the action. You are only on the receiving end. Often, an external curse comes from a place of anger and frustration to hurt someone who has hurt the cursor. In this case, it is a deliberate curse. External curses can both be deliberate or unconscious. Let's look at the differences.

A Deliberate Curse

To be cursed deliberately is quite rare. People are usually more self-centered. Most people will rather spend their time and energy on themselves than focusing on others. Cursing someone really takes a lot out of a person, as we discussed earlier. And as mentioned in the book already, not many magickians would render their services to curse someone as the price can be very high. So, for you to be deliberately cursed is often not the case.

But if you think you are deliberately cursed, do some introspection. Ask yourself whom you might have offended or angered at some point? Who would want some form of revenge against you? Try to find out if someone is jealous or envious of you. This allows you to either make amends or sever the connection from the source. However, as I've mentioned before, it's never a good idea to go on a "curse hunt" because eventually you might begin to perceive many things as "cursed" and place yourself in a victim mentality.

Most often, a curse will only be cast on people who truly deserve it and are wicked to the core. And even then, a skilled magickian would rather use binding spells or reversal spells that require far less effort and energy if a curse is suspected. Those who walk with anger and hatred in their hearts are vulnerable by cursing themselves anyway.

This book greatly deals with these types of curses and how to protect yourself. By understanding how the darker side of magick works and learning how to protect yourself, the magickian skillfully learns to use all the tools. Curses are real. For this reason, we have touched on all the aspects of protecting yourself and getting rid of negative energy. We have learned how to cleanse ourselves and put wards around us. Even if you feel you are deliberately cursed, there are skillful ways to deal with that.

External Curses Can Sometimes Be Cast Unconsciously

While deliberate curses are far rarer than most of us would like to admit, unconscious curses are abundant. This is because there are millions of people completely unaware of their ability to influence reality. They live reactive lives and go through their days in looped realities. They wake up and repeat the same actions day in and day out without ever consciously making any real "life decisions." These people are what many mystics refer to as "asleep." They are stuck within their illusions and are simply "going through the motions." However, this doesn't mean they don't have the ability to affect reality. Far from it, they can become curse machines if they go off the rails and fall into a negative headspace.

Imagine someone waking up, about to do the same thing they have been doing for the past few years in order to sustain a reality they aren't particularly "enthralled" with. Except, as the person gets out of bed, they step into dog poop—their pet had an upset stomach and decided to unburden itself in their room. Upon their waking moments, the person is already bombarded with a negative feeling, and simply allows that negative feeling to linger.

As the day progresses, the person continues to fumble little things, adding more anger and frustration to the mix. At some point, the person mutters to themselves in a disgruntled fashion, "It's going to be a terrible day!" as they get behind the wheel of their car. They drive, and because of the morning delays, they are now stuck in traffic with other people going through the same rush. Anger continues to build up in the person, as they need to drive carefully to avoid colliding with other drivers submerged in similar rage.

As the person reaches their work, their parking spot is taken and they are forced to drive a few blocks away to park their car. While walking to their work from the car lot, they get pooped on by a very unhealthy-looking pigeon. This takes the person's anger and frustration to 99%, and they are about to explode as they walk into the office. Blinded by their rage, they aren't able to see your bag lying on the floor and they tripped over it, spilling their coffee and throwing papers all over the office.

Their rage reaches a boiling point and they explode—cursing you, attacking your person, degrading you in front of everyone. Depending on how you react, you will either accept a part of their rage and frustration, their anger and disillusionment—or your wards will hold and you'll avoid any of the backlash. Of course, the scenario we painted is an extreme event, but there are millions of minor curses that happen in the same fashion. Sometimes, the person cursing you won't even say it to your face, but rather mutter it under their breath, envisioning your demise with high emotional charge.

Remember, when negative imaginings meet a high emotional charge, it is using the same manifesting principles of the law of intention—except in reverse. Similarly, if someone is unconsciously cursing you, it follows this exact same principle. Except, instead of a blessing, they are sending you curses. This is what we call "spillover" curses, which is why your wards are so important.

If your wards are down, you are vulnerable to unconsciously being cursed by others by being enveloped by their narrative. Nonetheless, being a magickian or being "energetically aware" also makes you vulnerable to attacks. Most people have a little conscious perception of the subtle energies in their environment. The skill of awareness and sensitivity has to be developed. The more you are aware of subtle energies, the brighter your inner flame grows and the more you are susceptible to attacks. The more you are seen by the "other."

Nevertheless, it's best not to jump to conclusions based on fear and ignorance. Become aware of what is happening so that spiritual techniques can determine the cause and how to deal with it. Don't allow these spillover influences to affect your life.

How Can You Protect Yourself Against Spillover Curses?

As a magickian, one of the first important lessons learned is mindfulness. A successful practitioner has to be aware of what is going on around and inside her or him. When you can maintain moment-to-moment awareness of your thoughts, feelings, surroundings, and bodily sensations, you are able to protect yourself against spillover curses.

Being mindful teaches you to not judge your own feelings and thoughts. It is better to focus on what is happening now rather than dwelling on the past or creating the future. If you are mindful of your current situations, you would be able to determine if it is your own negative thoughts that are undermining you, or if it is an influence from outside that is putting a spell on you.

You are in charge of giving attention to your thoughts, and if you detect that they are harmful to you, you alone can choose a different reality or to let them go. But when you realize you are in a loop, how do you change that? What do you do to break that negative thought pattern? How do you guard yourself against negative thoughts?

When harmful energy is at play, it might not always be conscious; it could be the spillover of day-to-day living. Things like arguments, the continuous violence on television, grief, stress, depression and more; they can all leave unbalanced energy in the environment that lingers like dust.

All thoughts are energy, too. And when someone directs a thought towards you, they are directing energy. Often, without expressing the thought loudly, your energy, mood, and strength can be affected if you are not centered in your own power. These shifts are typically very subtle, and if you aren't fully aware of their presence, they can influence your behavior.

One way to deal with this energy is to use a protection ritual. In this book, we have covered protection rituals at great length. Protection rituals are created to protect your mind and minimize other people's unconscious spillover energy. A protection ritual has a similar function as the ozone layer.

You create a selective membrane around your being where unconscious spillovers are trapped and burnt up.

Another way to maintain protection is by wearing protection amulets or setting up guardians or wards. This way, you are protected all the time. It is specifically helpful when you feel low on energy. The amulet or guardian will bounce off any negativity without you even realizing it. In fact, a strong protection protocol involves several different techniques and items—calculating even the unforeseen circumstances.

You can also create a mantra that you repeat daily when you sense negative energy. Create a mantra that helps you be mindful by asking questions like, "What am I spending my energy on right now?", "Is this helpful?", "What am I spending my attention on?", "Am I allowing myself to drift off?", "What doors do I unintentionally leave open or close?"

A good way to start your day is to practice a protection ritual. Meditate and focus on sharpening awareness. Teach yourself to detect lower-impulse thought patterns. It takes dedication and determination to shape your overall awareness. Remember, just as with other spells, a protection spell needs focus and intent to affect change. You are the agent of change. Repeating these rituals allows you to strengthen the wards and maintain a protective field around you. It's not enough to just cast it once and leave it as is. Every day, start with gratitude and build a hedge of light and love around you to operate at your optimal frequency. To do it sparingly will leave you vulnerable, and as anyone who's been under the oppression of darkness knows, a little bit of negativity can spiral into pandemonium.

In magick, we have the ability to create boundaries where energy is contained. By creating a sacred space, we block out unwanted energies and spirits. When we have our protective shield, it becomes less likely that you'll suffer at the hand of external curses. We have learned that protection rituals create a boundary between our lives and everything else, allowing us to operate under our conditions and not be subjected to the whims of others.

Yet, this is not the only source of curses—you, too, can be your own worst enemy. In the next section, we'll be exploring curses that come from yourself!

What Are Internal Curses?

We easily get "lost in thought" and, in turn, become reactive as opposed to proactive. If we are not mindful of the impact of negative thoughts, we can easily fall into a pit of despair. This is where we can ultimately believe that we are cursed. Know your own blind spots and learn how to be mindful of them.

When you are living in a reactionary state, your own emotions and train of thought corrupt the power of the law of attraction against you. What you put out there, comes back to you. This is one of the laws that practitioners know well. Therefore, if you expect a negative outcome, odds are that you're going to be proven right. If you believe you are never going to find love, you are not. You create your own cursed reality.

Again: NEGATIVE EVENT meets HIGH EMOTIONAL CHARGE mixed with VIVID VISUALIZATION creating UNWANTED SITUATIONS.

An example of this is when you receive a utility bill that is higher than expected. You know that you don't have enough money to pay for it now. Thus, you visualize how the electricity in your home will be cut, and you see yourself sitting in the dark without the internet and the ability to cook. This image, in turn, makes you wonder how you'll have to get the money, who you'll have to ask, what you'll have to do. Each scene paints a dreary picture where you have to face the fact you were incapable of paying the bill in the first place. This sparks the idea that perhaps you're "just not good enough" and "deserving of this" because of X, Y, and Z. Your anxiety levels spike, and when you couple this with the vivid visualizations you're doing in the moment, you're actually invoking those very elements you fear. The more fixated you are on the potential result, the more energy you give towards that situation and the less time you spend on mitigating damage or finding solutions. Even your solutions become problematic under this framing because you are the victim of the situation; that is, you're already accepting defeat before any of this outcome has ever happened. Depending on how much you feed these ideas creates the cursedness of your reality.

But just as you can create your own cursed reality, so you can create a different reality. Mindfulness, again, is a key component to alter your reality. By manifesting your victory, you need to be aware of your situation. Be mindful of these negative thoughts and how to deal with them. This doesn't mean you need to fake happiness or lie to yourself, but rather, it's about observing that which ails you and accepting it for what it is. To not judge it, but to simply acknowledge that it is present in this moment and how it makes you feel, but to ultimately become indifferent to it. That way, you remove the emotional charge from the negative situation and dismantle the cursed reality. This isn't about denying that which is uncomfortable, but learning to simply acknowledge that "this is how it is for now, but all things are in constant flux."

Thoughts are powerful. They can inspire you, motivate you, push you through hard times, or they can be heavy, energy-sapping, and limiting. If you are mindful of the nature of your thoughts, you are on your road to victory. You begin to take manual control over your own internal world and choose more resourceful states. Thoughts create energy that creates fields that either bring positive or negative results. You have the power to choose how this energy should manifest.

Just as a friendly reminder, you cannot get a positive result through a negative action. Only higher-vibrating actions produce higher-vibrating results.

For you to manifest your victory, you have to be mindful of your situation and your thoughts. Even if you know how to protect yourself and use protective rituals, you are not a hundred percent void of cursed realities. Negative energy can spill over and infect a particular aspect of your life. This spillover, in turn, can hinder other areas in your life, which eventually manifests into a "curse" or a structure of negativity unconsciously built by the mind. Mindfulness is a key component of protecting you against that.

In the book, there are various protection rituals. Use them to protect yourself. Create your own rituals based on what you learn. The more authentic your ritual, the more powerful it becomes. The more you grow in your practice of mindfulness, the easier it becomes. Your own mindfulness will create deliberate action to realign your reality. The more you practice and use your rituals as a tool, the easier it gets. Magick is accumulative, adding something more to the entire ritual every time you use it. Over time, rituals can become very powerful if you maintain a high emotional charge to them, and ascribe deep and holy meaning to them.

It's very important to remember to keep a balanced view of your situation. If you believe there is an issue that needs protection, analyze the situation to avoid drama and conflict. Balance brings stability that allows you to assess your situation. Something like the pentacle is a great tool to help you find balance.

How Can the Pentacle Help Bring Balance?

The pentacle, with its five points, serves as an awesome tool to bring balance in protection magick. The five elements work like this:

Earth – this is all about grounding. It teaches you to be practical and rational, and not to jump to conclusions about being cursed or attacked.

Water – with water, it's all about compassion. If you discover that someone is at the root of your situation, show compassion and sympathy to that person. People only hurt others when they are hurt. So, if you have hurt or harmed someone, show compassion regardless of whether you agree with it or not because it's still their own experience, so it will hold truth to them no matter what is true. Their actions are not excused, but with spiritual empathy, you will handle the situation with grace rather than anger.

Air – understanding the mechanics of subtle energy lets you understand the dynamics of self-defense. If you understand your own truths and how to use your gifts, your true self is protected against being hurt by others. Air is about your thoughts and ideas.

Fire – you have to claim your own personal power. This is the only way to be protected at all times. If you are centered in high ethical power and act responsibly, the Universe will support you and you will not be defeated. Fire represents your passions and motivations, your emotional charge.

Spirit – spirit and purpose go hand in hand. Everything has a purpose in the greater pattern of the universe. The mastery of our own purpose will constantly be challenged for us to evolve and master our own ideals of grounding, compassion, understanding, and power. This represents the unification of all of the elements, an elemental being—you!

When you're challenged, keeping to the principles of the protection pentacle will allow you to face any challenge with grace and compassion. One way is to invoke the pentacle around you like a shield; another is to create a pendant containing the pentacle, and another is to create a mantra to invoke a pentacle on the astral plane. It's important to really connect to each element, to invite them to form a hedge around you. This type of elemental invocation will open many doors for you as it acts as a sort of an "astral passport." You vibe at the same frequency as nature, and thus nature responds in kind.

Know It Is Not Always a Curse

We have to acknowledge the fact that it is not always a curse. As we have noticed in the above-mentioned sections, power lies within us. We are often our worst enemies. Often, our current condition is a result of a fear-based manifestation, and a fear-based manifestation creates undesired situations. If we focus on the negative, we give it fuel. If we don't actively engage in our situation because of fear, we are not acknowledging the current reality. The sooner we become aware of the situation, the sooner we will know how to handle it.

Our own fear can be a great teacher. But if you're constantly living in denial, or trying to intellectualize it, you are feeding negative energy. Ignoring a bad situation gives it time to get stronger. Eventually, you get trapped in that situation without realizing all you need to do is protect yourself. This is when it becomes so easy to mistake ordinary fear-based manifestations for a curse. Let us not look back in anger or forward in fear, but around us in awareness.

In witchcraft, you need to develop your intuition as well as your intellect to be able to discern which fears must be overcome and which fears must be embraced. Some fears have your best interest at heart. Experience is the best teacher. By dealing with your experiences, you move forward.

Fear is not the only thing that can keep you off the road. If there is any doubt in believing your instincts and intuition, it will result in a whirlpool of negative happenings. You have learned now that a spree of bad luck could mean you are cursed. But is that the truth? Is the curse real, or are you manifesting this cursed reality because of your own doubt?

Sometimes, what is happening to us is there to let us grow. Growth is uncomfortable. Our limits get pushed. We have to see how far we can go. Going beyond our limits always brings discomfort. And victory always lies on the other side of your limits. Rather than resisting the discomfort, embrace it. It's part of testing your character and resolving current issues you're struggling with. You may not be 100% aware of the growth that is happening in your life, but understand that it's your soul evolution happening now. This evolution is building character; however, this can only become beneficial when you stop resisting it, and rather, acknowledge its existence and observe yourself in contrast to it. Once you can detach emotionally from the externality and understand that it's just a lesson, you typically tend to transcend the situation rather quickly. Resist, and for sure it will persist until you accept it.

If you're not 100% certain that you are cursed or not, it's good to question. However, as we mentioned earlier, being fixated on the source of your curse can actually make it worse. Ignoring everything, on the other hand, is also not healthy. By using some form of divination, you can detect if you are being cursed. While divination should not be used as the main source of your decisions, it's good to use it when you need to do some "deeper questioning" of particular situations or people.

There are various forms of divination to direct you. We covered that in the book, too. To refresh your memory, look at the Pendulum, Tarot, Runes, or more to help discern your situation before arriving at the conclusion it is a curse, or simply a negative attitude that needs adjustment.

We are ultimately on earth for the evolution of our souls. We will constantly be tested and tried. To maintain true victory, you should accept the higher self's soul evolution for you. Here on earth is where your soul evolution takes place. This is because only on earth can you enter into these visceral challenges. Only here can you experience the struggle and suffering that is sometimes needed for growth. Your life is the playground for your growth. It's a single player game and you're the main character. Therefore, for growth to happen, you have to align yourself with your destiny and accept that some things might be uncomfortable at times. Through acceptance and alignment, every situation becomes a teacher and an opportunity. It's not always easy to adopt this way of thinking, but when you practice it enough, it becomes easier.

Use the basic foundations of protection magick to form your own rituals and spells. Make it personal and use them for self-empowerment. Learn to be mindful and perceptive. Learn to discern if it's a curse or a hex, or if it's just part of your walk. These are the tenants that you need to maintain yourself free from curses and the likes.

With your will, creativity, and knowledge, create your own protection magick. This is the ultimate purpose of this book: to open a door for your mind so you can use your own creative power to craft a mighty system based on your own innate designs.

CONCLUSION

The purpose of this book is to speak about protection and how to get rid of magickal, psychic, and spiritual attacks. It is something that happens every day, and could happen to anyone. Sometimes, it's not even done by fellow practitioners, but by major corporations and political parties. Where does a magickal seal of binding end and a corporate logo start? Where do NLP and shady advertising tricks in a sale end and where does spellbinding begin? Today, very advanced techniques of psychic manipulation are used against you to control your behavior daily. Social media has an infinite stream of people's consciousness bouncing against yours, everyone with an opinion about how life "should be."

Sometimes, you may be outgunned, overwhelmed, or just dealing with someone or something bigger than you. There is no shame in that, as Magick comes with years of experience. But if you ever are in a situation like this, ask for help. A good magickian knows when to reach out for assistance.

The idea behind this book is to help you put on armor to protect yourself against spells and curses. The idea is to create awareness of how to practice banishing and protection spells. All the tools and information in the book are to help you take back control and accomplish your goals. This is where any witch or warlock wants to be—free from the externalities and able to focus on their soul mission.

We touched on many different currents and spoke a little about them. We also saw that the purely traditional path is rarely in use anymore. Our modern lifestyle with its different forms of communication and travel has made the world smaller than before. We are now entering into some sort of hybridized fusion between technology and magick. The chances for different practitioners from different paths to meet up and learn from one another is very big. At the same time, all these different traditions of magick open the door to more attacks. With more eyes, there is more energy, and this is even more reason to be prepared. What might work as a defense against one might not work against another. This is why it is important to be informed and have an open mind. It's important to continuously maintain and modify your spells as you continue to advance in your life.

Magick works on many different levels. Different magickal traditions might focus on different angles or aspects of magick. Some might use spoken words while others might curse you with a text. And let's not even get started with Trolls! What was once fiction is now alive within the digital realm. In a world where you can encounter any type of magickal practitioner, it's necessary to defend yourself on all levels.

There are many ways to identify and mount a defense against the various types of magickal attacks that you are faced with. If you are still a beginner, there is no shame in seeking help from someone more experienced. However, for those who do not have the ability to seek out someone more experienced, this is why I wrote this book.

In this book, you will find specific spells for certain things and guidelines for others. Magickal attacks can be a horrifying experience. Learning how to defend and protect yourself is a valuable asset. With all the information out there, I hope this book will answer some of your questions and concerns. This book is meant to pique your interest.

The idea is to learn from this book, and form your own strategy and framework for dealing with attacks. Preparing yourself and being alert is very helpful as a practitioner of witchcraft. Everyone should be savvy in self-defense.

By practicing magick seriously, you get to know your own strengths and how to deal with serious issues. You learn when to cast protection spells, or when to bind or banish things or persons.

The last part of the book addresses aspects of walking in victory. Strengthen yourself by being consistent. Practice your mind and become aware of your surroundings on a spiritual and physical level. We covered means of initiation, expression, spell work, rituals, and much more. It is within the body of this work that your magick will grow. Your protection spells will be able to go beyond the constraints of self.

This is the ultimate call of the magickian: to go beyond self. We have the Great Work, and there are an infinite number of ways we can approach the topic of magick. Find what works best for you and use the spells in this book to forge something new. There is no limit to your greatness except for your belief about yourself.

Obviously, we approach magick with humility, lest we fly too close to the sun and burn our wings. Remember, consistency over time will allow you to go farther than you've ever dreamed of.

It's one thing to learn how to protect yourself and stay alert. But it's another thing to maintain that victory.

Be blessed on your path, and may your magick protect you!

Last message and small request from the Magickal Witches team:

We wish you nothing but magickal success and health on your journey of being a powerful witch! If you've enjoyed this book or found that it has been exactly what you've needed, please consider leaving the book a review here where you can find the book in Glinda Porter's author profile. You will also find all her other literature that you'd love to check out. We're sure of it!

All feedback is extremely important to us because it helps us deliver exactly what you want and it also helps other readers make a decision when deciding on the best books to purchase. We would greatly appreciate it if you could take 60 seconds to leave the book a quick review. You can also reach out via email to leave any feedback.

Email: magick@magickalwitches.com

Website: www.magickalwitches.com

Author   Profile: https://www.amazon.com/author/glindaporter

Lastly, don't forget to claim the "Survival and Wellness Kit for Magickal Witches" by scanning the QR code to receive:

- 10 Elixirs For Detoxification and Aura Cleansing

- 12 Spell Jar Recipes For Protection

- Guide For Talisman Preparation For Use Outside Home

- 20 Daily Detox Tips To Keep Your Vessel Clear

- Master Ingredient Shopping List

Resources

Books-, -P.
(2021). *By Jason Miller: Protection and Reversal Magick (Beyond 101)*
(7301st ed.). Paperback.

Connolly, S.
(2021). *Curses, Hexes & Crossing: A Magician's Guide to Execration Magick by S. Connolly (2011–04-14).* CreateSpace Independent Publishing
Platform.

Dugan, E.
(2011). *Practical Protection Magick: Guarding & Reclaiming Your Power.*
Llewellyn Publications.

K, A., & K,
A. A. (2010). *How to Become a Witch: The Path of Nature, Spirit & Magick*
(Illustrated ed.). Llewellyn Publications.

Kraig, D. M.
(2010). *Modern Magick: Twelve Lessons in the High Magick-*

al Arts
(Expanded ed.). Llewellyn Publications.

Malbrough, R. T.
(2009). *Charms, Spells, and Formulas for the Making and Use of Gris-Gris,*
(1987th, 3rd Printing ed. ed.). Llewellyn Publications.

Marden, O. S.
(2020). *The Victorious Attitude.* Independently published.

McCarthy, J.
(2018). *Magical Healing: A Health Survival Guide for Magicians and Healers.*
Apocryphile Press.

Morrison, D.,
& Blackthorn, A. (2020). *Utterly Wicked: Hexes, Curses, and Other*
Unsavory Notions. Weiser Books.

Penczak, C.
(n.d.). *The Witch's Shield Publisher: Llewellyn Publications.*
Llewellyn
Publications.

Published, I.
(2008). *Breaking Curses, Including Generational Curses.* Independently
published.

Rowe, B. (1999).
The Essential Skills of Magick. Independently published.

Scanlon, S. M.
(2012). *Everything You Want to Know About Magick: But Were Afraid to Ask.*
Llewellyn Publications.

Shadrach, N.
(2014). *Magic That Works: Practical Training for the Children of Light.*
Ishtar Publishing.

Telesco, P.
(1999). *Magick Made Easy: Charms, Spells, Potions and Power* (1st ed.). HarperOne.

Made in the USA
Monee, IL
05 July 2025

20549231R00111